TREASURE

A SEAFORD ANTHOLOGY

The Beach Seaford Looking East

Compiled and introduced

by

Diana Crook

Diana Crook

Dale House Press

For Kevin Gordon,

who taught me about the history of Seaford

Published by Dale House Press,
100 Marine Parade, Seaford BN25 2QR

ISBN: 978-1-900841-06-1

British Library Cataloguing-in-Publication Data.
A catalogue record for this book is available from the British Library

Printed and bound by 4Edge, 7A Eldon Way, Hockley, Essex SS7 2DA

Contents

Foreword

Seaford has a rich history, ranging from its influential days as a Cinque Port and rotten borough to today's modern seaside resort where battle still continues to contain the ravages of the sea.

This anthology does not attempt to be a history of Seaford, but rather gathers together a collection of interesting, entertaining or unusual pieces that give a flavour of the town through the centuries. The influence of the sea is felt throughout, with dramatic stories of sea battles, wrecks, looting and smuggling, and the heroism of those who risk its fury.

The villages of Bishopstone and East Blatchington are included in the anthology because their location and history are so closely intertwined with that of Seaford, but I have resisted the temptation to stray any further afield. Some of the handwritten documents researched have been difficult to read, and I apologise for any errors in transcription. I have indicated where a word is illegible [?] or my interpretation doubtful [word?].

In the interests of authenticity, old or outdated spellings and the unnecessary use of capital letters have been retained. To make the book easy to read, I have avoided footnotes and put relevant details in square brackets and individual item headings in italics. Extracts are as far as possible chronological, and the source is dated only if the text requires it – fuller details are given in the bibliography. This list of books may tempt readers to delve further into the story of Seaford, but above all else I hope they will enjoy rifling through this treasure chest.

Diana Crook
May 2012

Acknowledgements

I am deeply indebted to Seaford Museum and its chairman Kay Turvey for generously allowing me to research the archives and quote numerous extracts. The East Sussex Record Office has been similarly generous, and its search room staff were impressively patient with my many requests. I am grateful to all those authors and publishers who have given me permission to quote from their books. Joan Astell, Zöe Ford, Rodney Castleden, Reg Dove, Peter Fellows, Mary Lowerson, David Swaysland, Paul Waller, Sue Sutton and Dick Richardson of Country Books have all been particularly helpful, as has Kevin Gordon, who also kindly gave up his time to check my typescript for any historical howlers.

The Sussex Archaeological Society library helped me find various items, and the staff at Seaford Library went out of their way to assist while busy with new premises. My husband John has, as always, extricated me from my losing battles with the software, and David Arscott has been both expert and patient in preparing the book for publication.

The illustrations in the book are of early twentieth century postcards from my personal collection.

THE TOWN

For and against

Ford Madox Heuffer (as Kent man Ford Madox Ford used to be called) declared it was the incorporation of Pevensey and Seaford into the Cinque Ports in the sixteenth century that established the county's reputation for stupidity. He could have been right.
Judy Moore, *Silly Sussex*

Like all the towns along the Sussex coast, Seaford suffered repeatedly from the attacks of the French in the fourteenth and fifteenth centuries; documents dated 1342 say that the parish had been damaged often and one dated 1357 makes it clear that the town had been devastated. The latter document shows that the French were not the only despoilers, as it is an injunction giving orders to the bailiffs to stop one James Archer completing the demolition of the town in order to sell the building materials. A patent for building a wall was granted in 1322 but was apparently never acted upon.
Fred Aldsworth and David Freke, *Historic Towns in Sussex*

Feuds in the Town. From the time of Elizabeth till the beginning of the present century, the town was remarkable for the personal hostility of many of its inhabitants.
MA Lower & WD Cooper, *Further Memorials of Seaford*, 1865

Mon 7 June 1756 ... Seaford is a small town with many good buildings in and near it, but it doth not stand compact, for the houses are very much separated. It lies about half a mile from the sea, and upon the cliff near the sea is built a sort of fort, but no guns in it, nor in reality is it of any service, for it lies so much higher than the sea that I think they could not point the guns to do any great execution; and the walls, being built of flint, and so very thin, that if a cannon of any large weight were fired against it, I think the flints must of consequence destroy all the men in the fort. Between the town and fort there are 4 18-pounders laid, which, I think, if rightly ordered, might be of signal service in war-time to protect their fishery from the insults of privateers...

The Diary of Thomas Turner, 1754–1765

Like other places on the southern coast, which until lately were but inconsiderable fishing stations, Seaford has felt the impulse of fashion, and become a retired, but in many respects, an agreeable sea bathing place. In early times it was doubtless a town of more consequence than its present condition would seem to indicate.

TW Horsfield, *The History of Sussex*, 1835

The town of Seaford is rich in historical and archaeological interest. Although its population is reduced to less than 1000 inhabitants, and although its electoral privileges   as ancient as any in the realm – were swept away by the Reform Act, it still retains municipal rights, and is governed by a Bailiff and Jurats. And although despoiled of its port by the operation of natural causes, it is not without ample *vestigia* of those days when it occupied a respectable position in the political and commercial affairs of the kingdom.

MA Lower, *Memorials of Seaford*, SAS VII, 1854

SEAFORD (population 997), a member of the Cinque Port of Hastings, is probably the ancient Mercredesburn (Mœr-cryd, the sea-ford), the site of Saxon Ella's victory in 485. It stands on the right bank of the Cuckmere. The old town was placed on the marge of the haven – formed by the junction of the Ouse with the Channel – which has been long filled up. The position, however, of the modern hamlet, with a bold sweep of sea before it, and lofty hills rearing their rounded crests behind it, is so picturesque that we may anticipate for it a long and prosperous career.

Black's Guide to Sussex, 1861

Brighton – Queen of Watering Places – Hastings, Scarborough, Torquay, Ramsgate, Ryde, Dawlish, St Leonard's, Weston-super-Mare, Worthing, Eastbourne, Llandudno, Margate, will please to keep silence while I rehearse the manifold advantages of this little sea-side resort, remarkable for the salubrity of its climate, the romantic beauty of its scenery, the quietness of its surroundings, the snug comfort of its simple lodgings, and the civility of its townsmen. It possesses none of the glitter and glare of more fashionable resorts, there are no splendid equipages in its streets; no long lists of fashionable arrivals in the newspapers; no grand libraries and lounging-rooms; no ceremonious introductions; nothing, in short, that need interfere with the perfect calm which is the desideratum of the overworked student, the valetudinarian, the quiet observer of the beauties of nature, the geologist, the sea-angler, the pedestrian, or the lover of horse exercise on the free open down.

MA Lower, *Notes on Seaford*, 1868

Then he [visitor] will behold one of the most charming scenes on the southern coast. The Bay, with its sweep of several miles, in its various phases of ocean calm and billow; the opposite cliffs of Newhaven, with steamers and sailing craft, approaching or leaving the harbour; the low lands in the foreground, flanked by the cheerful-looking town, with its old grey church in the middle distance; more to the right the picturesque village and church of Blatchington, embosomed in trees, and a grey background of hills stretching away to Mount Harry, behind Lewes – form, in the ensemble, a picture of no ordinary interest or beauty.

W Banks, *Seaford: Past and Present. Handbook and Visitors' Guide*, 1892

The town was aiming to imitate Brighton, but the entrepreneurial Seaford Bay Estate Company had overlooked the rigours of Seaford's winter gales and their few seaside homes and lodgings were never to prove commercially viable.

The Company's proposed developments were very grandiose and the whole area from Splash Point to the present end of Dane Road was planned on the lines of Brighton with 12 parallel roads of terraced houses running back in serried rows from the Esplanade to College Road and Steine Road [sic] only relieved by a miniature 'Royal Crescent' on the centre line of the Martello Tower. Behind this, Cricket Field was to be flanked on the north and east by 22 seaside bungalows (of three storeys!), nine of which were actually built before the company went bankrupt and any further permanent development subsided under the threat and eventual demands of the Great War.

John Odam, *Bygone Seaford*

When, in October 1917, I first went to Seaford, it was very different from the lively place it has now become. The 'development' of the Front had been nipped in the bud in 1914, and many acres of rough, untidy ground were left lying in neglected ugliness.

Agnes H Carter, *A Canteen in a Canadian Camp* (1917), SCM Vol 8, 1934

> The busy streets, the merry throng,
> Enrapture each new comer;
> Save for one awkward contretemps
> So recent as last summer;
>
> Bathers unclothed (a shocking sight!)
> The Esplanade invaded;
> The crimson blushes have not quite
> From Seaford cheeks yet faded.
>
> Nay, turn to yonder bowling green, -
> Its players skilled yet gentle.
> Where never act nor word has been
> To morals detrimental.
>
> And lo! When youth surveys, austere,
> His middle-aged relations,
> Good Seaford calls him – 'Bring them here,
> Remote from *all* temptations!'

Edith CM Boodle, extract from *Seaford*, SCM Vol 1, 1927

SEAFORD. The chief attraction for Visitors to Seaford is its restful environs. Placed on a gentle southern slope, between the sea and Downs, it has a South-west aspect, mild climate suitable alike to old and young and enjoys a high average amount of sunshine. The health of the town is phenomenal: many London Physicians speak highly of the air and surroundings as of wonderful recuperative effect to the brain fagged and nerve weary.

Sunny Seaford, Official Publicity Bureau, 1936

SEAFORD. God made it beautiful, and man has not entirely spoiled it. The massive white walls of the Downs are still as they have been a million years, and not even the mess that men have made of Seaford's three-mile front can rob them of their glory. East of the town is Seaford Head, with a prehistoric camp and Roman graves. From it is a noble view of the Downs, with the majestic Seven Sisters cliffs unsurpassed on the English coast...

Arthur Mee, *Sussex*, 1937

But Sussex has another treasure of a different nature in her many delightful villages and hamlets, small manor-houses and farmsteads, scattered about the county. It is practically useless to look for these along the coast – any core of decent old building between Brighton and Littlehampton, where the alluvial plain comes down to the sea, is smothered and hidden in modern slums. And to the eastwards as well there is the shoddy Peacehaven and the ruined Seaford. Most of the Sussex coast, except where it is actual chalk cliff, is shabby and out-at-elbows, littered as if with a giant child's cheap toys.

Esther Meynell, *Sussex*, 1945

It seems strange that Seaford was once one of the Cinque Ports; not merely because the harbour was displaced when the channel shifted to Newhaven, but more because the name 'Cinque Port' is full of romance, while Seaford is only an unattractive seaside resort. It is, however, near to some pleasant places.

Reginald Turnor, *Sussex*, 1947

Seaford is the least gay of the chain of south coast seaside places s[outh] of London. It has no pavilion, no amusement arcade, and a short ESPLANADE, which, at the time of writing, appears far from thriving. There is the ESPLANADE HOTEL, neat and quite large, of 1907. To its right a decaying terrace, to its left a substantial Gothic one, probably of about 1875. The east end is the MARTELLO TOWER of 1810 with a Victorian top.

Ian Nairn and Nikolaus Pevsner, *Sussex, The Buildings of England*, 1965

Another notable failure was Seaford. This decayed port rapidly acquired all the trappings of a resort. By 1798 it provided as good a range of facilities as the larger watering-places – hot and cold baths, assemblies, lodging houses and even a small 'wilderness' for the recreation of its visitors. Yet it was plainly an over-development, and the temporary decline in bathing which followed the resumption of normal traffic with the continent after 1815 killed Seaford's ambitions. Its present townscape is largely Victorian and Edwardian and its rebirth was due to the growing numbers of retired people settling in the town later in the nineteenth century.
Peter Brandon, *The Sussex Landscape*, 1974

'Falling in love with Seaford was like falling in love with an ugly woman.'
WA Darlington [Bishopstone resident and long-time theatre critic of the *Daily Telegraph*.]

12   SEAFORD. — *The Esplanade.* — LL.

BUILDINGS

Domestic, Commercial and Military

STUART CALLF & CO. Terminus Buildings, Seaford. House Agents, Auctioneers, Surveyors. Furnished houses from $3^{1}/_{2}$ guineas. Building Land from £2 per foot. Houses for sale, £600 to £3,000. Phone 185.
Sunny Seaford, Official Publicity Bureau, 1936

The Crypt

Beneath a building known as the Folly, and situated in a yard at the back of Mr H Green's Premises in Church Street, is to be seen this very ancient structure. Unfortunately there are no records to show when it was built, or for what purpose. Evidence certainly is not wanting to show that at one time it must have been used for religious service. Probably the chapel of some ancient town guild. Tradition says that at one time the Court House of Seaford stood on the site.
WR Wynter, *Old Seaford*, 1922

Now known as Seaford's oldest surviving secular edifice, the box-like flint-walled building had for years received scant care or attention, save only from the likes of Mr MA Lower and Mr WR Wynter, writing almost a century ago, and members of Seaford Museum in the 1970s.

An imaginative scheme to erect a modern masonry 'shell' to enclose the entire original, with internal space between for exhibitions and lectures, came true in 1994; today the Crypt Gallery is in frequent use for art, craft and photographic displays and a variety of meetings and small social gatherings.
Patricia Berry, *Seaford Memories 1950–1999*

The house was originally built at Wellingham in the parish of Ringmer, by a man named Whitfield, who was largely connected with the contraband trade, and was an importer of Corsica wine. Having been outlawed for the offence, he is said to have got his outlawry reversed by the simple but somewhat impudent expedient of presenting the King (George II) with some of his choicest samples of the prohibited wine! On this account the mansion acquired the sobriquet of Corsica Hall. After Mr Whitfield's decease it was occupied by Francis, 5th Lord Napier, and during his tenancy became the scene of a painful domestic tragedy.

In the month of May, 1772, one of his lordship's sons, a little boy, in a frolicsome humour took up a loaded pistol that had inadvertently been left upon the table at which the Rev Mr Loudon, his lordship's domestic chaplain, was sitting, and aiming it at him said, 'Shall I shoot you?' to which the reverend gentleman laughingly replied, 'Shoot on!' The child pulled the trigger and Mr Loudon fell dead upon the floor… From the period of this tragical event Corsica Hall was invested by the ignorant and superstitious with an evil and unlucky character, and after the death of Lord Napier no tenant could be found for it. It was therefore advertised for sale, and the materials were purchased by a clock and watch maker of Lewes, named Harben, who, according to popular rumour, had become suddenly rich in consequence of his having purchased, as base metal, some of the golden spoils of the celebrated wreck of the *Nympha Americana*, which took place near Beachy Head, in 1747. Mr Harben removed Corsica Hall to its present site, and became a person of influence in the town.

MA Lower, *Memorials of Seaford,* 1854

Harben's son, Thomas, had 13 children and two of them deserve mention. One daughter, Susan, became Matron of the School in Yorkshire which the Brontë sisters attended, and, in Charlotte's Jane Eyre Susan Harben formed the basis for the character Mrs Harden, 'made up of equal parts of whalebone and iron'. One of Thomas's sons had 18 children, and one, Caroline, married and became mother of Joseph Chamberlain who, as conservative MP for Birmingham, split the Tory party asunder between 1903 and 1906 on the issue of tariffs. But his son, Neville, the great, great, great grandson of the man who brought Corsica Hall to Seaford, became Prime Minister from 1937 to 1940. His policies of 'appeasement' and his tragic failure to understand the true nature of Hitler must be held largely responsible for the outbreak of war in 1939.

It seems ironic that, in Seaford, a small town so greatly affected by that terrible conflict, we should trace the ancestry of the Prime Minister who finally declared war on Germany...

Edna and Mac McCarthy, *History Trail of the Town and Cinque Port of Seaford*

Martello Tower [now the Seaford Museum]

> The Martello's relict canon
> Stands impotent guard
> Over cappuccinos, choc-ices,
> Pastel beach huts,
> And on this sun-shone afternoon
> Repels melancholy.

Peter Martin, extract from *Ghost Music*

This tower was built on the beach at Seaford about 1801, during the time of the threatened invasion of England by Bonaparte. It is the largest and most westward on the coast. The base forms a circle of 136 feet in circumference, tapering upwards to a circumference of 90 feet at the top. The height is 32 feet, built in brick and coped with large blocks of granite. The wall facing the sea is over six feet in thickness. The tower contained a magazine and accommodation for an officer and 34 men. Surrounded by a deep fosse, faced by a wall of solid brickwork, and crossed by a drawbridge. The cost of the building was about £18,000, and the bricks used in the construction numbered something like 50,000 for the completion of a single course, or a total of about two and a quarter millions.

WR Wynter, *Old Seaford*

Military Defences – The Martello Tower, No 74, the westernmost of the series, stands on the beach opposite the south-eastern quarter of the town. Like its brethren, it is a low circular structure, with a wide moat, and drawbridge, and mounts one swivel cannon. It is now almost useless.

MA Lower, *Notes on Seaford*, 1868

What to See in Seaford,
For Twopence

THE
M A R T E L L O   T O W E R
NO 74

Built about the year 1800 at a cost of £18,000 this Tower was purchased in 1911 by T Funnell and is opened up more than any other one along the coast. In converting it into an Open Air Skating Rink and Tea Rooms (and proposed Sea Water Baths), it was necessary to cut three holes through walls seven feet thick.

The Moat is 360 feet round and contains 10,000 square feet of skating surface. A fine cement staircase and chimney piece has been constructed. The Magazine with its fourteen feet-thick walls and the old fresh water tank can still be seen.

In the Tower is to be seen one of the most wonderful inlaid table tops in the world (made by T. Funnell, the proprietor), which occupied thirteen years (evenings) to construct, and which was awarded a bronze medal and diploma at the Crystal Palace 1911. Over 20,000 pieces of wood of ten varieties were used.

THE TOWER IS THE COOLEST PLACE IN SEAFORD FOR TEAS
Pot of Tea, Roll and Butter – 5d
To View the Tower Only – 2d

Advertisement/poster c 1920, SMA

There's no precious hands-off policy here but an infectious philosophy of communal sharing. In any case, many of the objects were built to last – sturdy old radio sets, heavy typewriters, vacuum cleaners, lavatory bowls, commodes.

Humble items make an interesting display when collected in quantity. After the museum had been given enough cast-off spectacles to fill a large box, a local optician took them away and did a little homework. The result is a fascinating exhibit showing the changes in styles over the years. Similarly, there are displays of coins, embroidery, writing implements and much more...

The town's long history is briefly told, but the emphasis is on Seaford within living memory. When the Ritz cinema closed, for example, the museum secured its projectors and some of its display materials. And if you're only just coming to terms with computers it's a chastening thought that the early ones are already museum pieces. There are several here, including the first ever introduced to Seaford.

David Arscott, *Explore Sussex, Its Coast, Countryside and Heritage*, 1986

'My favourite museum in the world was the Seaford Museum which is a collection of rusty electronics under the Martello Tower on Seaford seafront.'

Grayson Perry interviewed on *Front Row*, BBC Radio 4, March 2009

Tide Mills

...in 1698 the main river mouth was near the marshland. The conception of a Tide Mill, a mill for the grinding of corn into flour, operated by the action of the tide, was the idea of the Duke of Newcastle, of Bishopstone Place...In 1761 the Duke secured the passage of a Bill through Parliament permitting three merchants, John Woods, William Woods and John Challenor, to erect one or more Tide Mills for grinding corn or grain, in the Parish of Bishopstone. By then the river's mouth was at Newhaven, but the creek to Tide Mills obviously still filled with water at high tide.

The village and industrial enterprise was later leased by William Catt. He controlled the area eastwards to the Buckle Inn, and supplies were delivered there by water borne barges. Large areas of marshland were drained, and earthen banks were constructed. Cottages, blacksmith's and carpenter's shops, Mill Offices and a granary, provided for a village population of about a hundred, families of mill workers and agricultural workers.

Edna and Mac McCarthy, *Sussex River, Seaford to Newhaven*

This is one of the most extensive works of the kind in the south of England. The houses connected with them form a kind of colony and include a pleasant residence, with beautiful gardens, a conservatory etc.

MA Lower, *Notes on Seaford*, 1868

Former residents tend to romanticise Tidemills, but few modern families would tolerate the conditions. Apart from the Mill buildings, blacksmith's and carpenter's shops, and granary there was a large barn and a small outhouse containing a communal mangle, another containing coppers for boiling clothes, and a small drying ground. Families arranged turns to boil clothes, and to use the mangle and the drying ground. Copper sticks, used to lift hot washing from the coppers, had other uses as the children of Tidemills sometimes discovered rather painfully.

The cottages, many built from Sussex boulder flints and having interesting lattice work porchways, were outwardly attractive... but there was no running water, and sanitation consisted of outside earthen closets. Several families shared outside water taps, and all water needed had to be carried into and out of the houses. There was no refuse collection and rubbish had to be carried out and dumped into one of several large, brick lined pits. Indoor lighting was by candles, or by oil lamps, but tallow candles were frequently washed ashore so that a cheap source of lighting was often available. Coal was stored in cellars under the stairs.

Edna and Mac McCarthy, *Sussex River, Seaford to Newhaven*

Thus the mill was built and worked for many years. It was a feature of interest in the neighbourhood and in East Sussex generally. It amply fulfilled the intention of its originators, and its purpose as set forth in the Act of Parliament.

Many years ago Mr Woolgar, an old man, a retired blacksmith, and a well-known inhabitant of Seaford, told me that he could remember that twice a week a large wagon drawn by four splendid horses travelled with flour for the King's troops as far as Portsmouth...

The Rev Frederick Willett, *The Tide-Mill, Bishopston*

Parts of the old mill village were taken over in 1922 for another venture that was in advance of its time – a convalescent hospital for injured race horses. This was set up by David Dale, who converted the old coal yard into loose boxes, while the mill house was used by stable employees. The horses came from all over the country and there were up to 30 at a time. Dale administered his special sea-water treatment on horses with weak fetlocks and similar complaints. Among the facilities was a huge tank of salt water, in which the horses were bathed in the belief that the salt helped them to recover from their injuries and strengthen their legs. They were also galloped along the seashore and sometimes led through the waves with a rein secured to a rowing boat.

Dale's enterprise lasted until the outbreak of the 1939-45 War and he earned a reputation for the great success of some of his cures.

Tidemills, A Village Ahead of Its Time, Seaford Museum & Heritage Society Publication.

RACING SCENES
SERIES OF 48   Nº 47

SEA BATH
Sea air and sea bathing are good for horses as well as for humans, and exercising in shallow sea water is especially good for horses with weak legs. These are a common and serious defect with racehorses, and the trainer David Dale has cured many apparently hopeless cases of leg trouble by sea treatment at Seaford. The sands are still used for an occasional irregular race meeting, and regularly for training during the hard weather.

ISSUED BY
GALLAHER LTD
VIRGINIA HOUSE, LONDON & BELFAST

SEA BATH

Breweries

At the end of the nineteenth century a major brewing force from Brighton, Tamplin & Sons Ltd, made their presence felt in Seaford. In 1899 they purchased from the son of William Catt, Henry Willett owner of the West Street Brewery, Brighton (formerly Vallance & Catt 1840-1890) twenty-one public houses. Therefore, the old 'Terminus Hotel'/'Station Inn' was part of their ever expanding empire. In 1901 the 'Crown' in Church Street joined this combine and later they were to take an interest in the unattached 'Buckle Inn'. So, with the Lewes Brewers dominating the market by owning the other five hostelries (Ballard & Co Ltd four and Beard's one) the stranglehold was complete. On top of this a change of management was in the air at the Seaford Bay Hotel which would finally sever the Brewery's last link here. No longer would the Elm Brewery be required...

Joan EV Redman, *A Pint Pot of Old Seaford*

Esplanade Hotel [destroyed by fire 1976]

The sea-front Esplanade Hotel, built in 1891 (with the five-storey west wing added three years later) as the crowning glory of the developers' plans for Seaford to rival Brighton, never recovered from the change in fashions both before and after the Second World War. By the 1960s, some of its busiest times were the Sunday luncheons served to visiting parents, bringing their sons and daughters out for the day from their nearby boarding schools. Some local organisations continued to hold annual dinners and other social occasions at the hotel, and location shots for one or two feature films were made there but the building grew shabby and forlorn – a far cry from the establishment that welcomed King Edward VII (plus pet terrier Caesar) in 1905.

Patricia Berry, *Seaford Memories 1950–1999*

Chyngton Estate

What was significant about the subsequent development on the estate at Seaford was the lack of ribbon development, and stipulations imposed on each of the 195 plots regarding minimum cost of various types of housing resulted in an orderly zoning of working-class dwellings, 'artistic villas' and shops on the lower slopes, and provision for 'superior' detached houses on the upper. Only one private detached or semi-detached house was to be erected on plots of 50ft frontage. No hotels, public houses, beer-shops, asylums, letting houses, caravans or temporary buildings, or any traders or businesses (including 'blacksmith, bell-hanger, gasfitter, locksmith, tinman or slaughterman') were permitted, with the exception of certain shops in the working-class areas. The building programme began soon after the end of the war and was largely completed by 1939. Some parts were built later, but they always conformed to the original proposals of 1914.

Peter Brandon, *The Discovery of Sussex*

The Buckle Inn [demolished and replaced 1963]

Tom [Venus] keeps the Buckle Inn, Bishopstone, near Newhaven – the loneliest inn on the south coast. When the gales blow, the narrow road outside is often sea-swept, at high tide it is almost awash.

Often traffic has to be diverted inland and the lamp in Tom's window shines in vain for local custom. Tom has known the coast, man and boy, more than 50 years. For three generations his family have lived at the Buckle, 400 years old and once the haunt of smugglers.

Tom has never known the windows to be opened. Neither have they been cleaned. 'It isn't worth the trouble, because the sea dirties them immediately.'

Evening News, 1949. SMA (housing register)

…a unique emergency scheme operated whenever high seas made the coast road impassable. The landlord of the old Buckle Inn, on judging the moment had come, would activate an illuminated sign placed well in advance of the junction, advising drivers to approach Seaford by an alternative (inland) route.

…The old Buckle was close enough to the sea that waves from rough high tides could momentarily submerge the building, washing water and shingle down the chimneys which the occupants then swept out through the front door.

Patricia Berry, *Seaford Memories 1950–1999*

Telsemaure [corner of Dane Road and Esplanade, demolished 1937]

Telsemaure was grand indeed, certainly by Seaford standards of the time. It was built with double outer walls and had eight bedrooms, four reception rooms and two bathrooms. There was also a play-room and, at the back of the house, a long school room running parallel to Dane Road... The bedrooms were fitted with mahogany furniture and massive bedsteads with goose-feather mattresses and pillows. The drawing room had walnut furniture and there was also a dining room and a library with more than 400 books. This was obviously a house of music as there were two pianos and an American organ with 42 stops. Other entertainment included a 'Kalloscope' which was a stereoscopic picture viewer...

The name Telsemaure is unique, each letter representing the first names of members of the [Crook] family, Thomas, Elizabeth, Lewis etc...

Kevin Gordon, *From a Seaford Album*, Sussex Express, 15th June, 2007

The House on the Beach

The house on the beach had been posted where it stood one supposes, for the sake of the sea-view, from which it turned right about to face the town across a patch of grass and salt scurf, looking like a square and scornful corporal engaged in the perpetual review of a squad of recruits. Sea delighted it not, nor land either. Marine Parade fronting it to the left, shaded sickly eyes, under a worn green verandah, from a sun that rarely appeared, as the traducers of spinsters pretend those virgins are ever keenly on their guard against him that cometh not. Belle Vue Terrace stared out of lank glass panes without reserve, unashamed of its yellow complexion. A gaping public house, calling itself newly Hotel, fell backward a step. Villas with the titles of royalty and bloody battles claimed five feet of garden and swelled in bow windows beside other villas which drew up firmly, commending to the attention a decent straightness and unintrusive decorum in preference. On an elevated meadow to the right was the Crouch. The hall of Elba nestled among weather-beaten dwarf woods further toward the cliff. Shavenness, feature-lessness, emptiness, clamminess, scurfiness, formed the outward expression of a town to which people were reasonably glad to come in the summer time, for there was nothing in Crikwswich [Seaford] to distract the naked pursuit of health.

George Meredith, *Short Stories, The House on the Beach*, 1920

Schools

'Mrs Beard takes the opportunity of informing the nobility and gentry that, at the desire of her friends, she proposes on Michaelmas next [1784] or soon after to remove her school to Seaford. Her superintendence of the education of young ladies during her long residence at Brighthelmston will, she hopes, be sufficient apology for favours and patronage of an impartial public. The sanitary air of Seaford and the convenience and accommodation for bathing and its retirement give it a decided superiority from point of situation to almost any other spot in Sussex. Many insuperable objections having been made to a place of public resort and amusement for female tuition. Attention to the different degrees of exterior improvement, the morals and health of the young ladies who are entrusted to her care and tenderness will be the essential objects of all her endeavours. The terms are 18 guineas for them that do not bathe and 26 guineas for Parlour Boarders and to find their washing and tea.'

Joan A Astell, *To the Independent Electors of Seaford*, 1768–1886

Seaside Education, Seaford, Sussex
Mr Mark Antony Lower, MA, FSA
Receives into his care two or three Pupils to prepare for the various examinations, and for active life in its several departments
Seaford offers every facility for Sea Bathing and careful Medical treatment. Gentlemen whose early education has been imperfect will find with Mr Lower the advantages of a strict educational oversight, combined with those of a comfortable home
References to many gentlemen of high literary attainment and social position
Terms, 100 and 120 Guineas Per Annum.

Frontispiece advertisement to *Notes on Seaford*, 1868, by MA Lower [Mr Lower lived at 6 Pelham Terrace]

1895 5th November. I have beguiled the children to school this afternoon by a promise of fireworks to be let off in play time.

1897 5th July. I have admitted Eustace Yeo today, he is in his tenth year and knows simply nothing, having been prevented from attending school through extreme delicacy.

1899 16th January. School re-opened after eight weeks of extra holiday on account of the prevalence of the fever.

1907 24th May. Empire Day. We celebrated this occasion as loyally as possible by learning and singing the National Anthem, by decorations with bunting, stories of Victoria the Good, a procession in the playground etc.

1909 12th March. We have sold over 100 slates at a penny each to the children…

1911 20th January. Measles are on the increase. About 50 children absent today.

1915 1st December. A great many West Indian Troops are in camp here and we have been visited by several soldiers, two of whom are schoolmasters from British Guyana and Trinidad.

1918 20th December. Mr C Pettitt is giving the children a splendid treat this afternoon, the first they have had since the commencement of the Great War. It is to be followed by the advent of Father Christmas who will distribute presents.

1919 21st July. The Prizes for Peace celebrations were presented here this afternoon. Mr Thornton presented all the little ones with a pretty 'Peace' cap. Mrs Morling sent a large supply of biscuits and sweets and Miss Ashby presented each child with a beautiful white handkerchief embroidered with the Allies flags.

1922 8th March. A terrible gale is raging today, such as one has not visited this coast for 25 years. In consequence 101 children are absent.

1928 31st October. I sincerely regret to state that I am relinquishing the post of Head Teacher in this School today after thirty-nine years of very happy work.

Miss Amy Chambers, *Log Book 1890–1928*. Infants School, Church Street, Seaford. SMA (Schools)

The blueprint of Britain's future homes is being drawn at Seaford. There, in a stately white house overlooking the sea, women teachers are learning how to plan, manage and run a home, how to sew, how to cook and how to look after an ordinary family and an ordinary house... Housecraft is a new word simply because the whole idea is new. Our daughters are no longer going to learn only the science of the job. No longer is a home to mean only so many this-or-that aspects and good or bad damp courses. No longer is laundry the art of folding a pocket-handkerchief exactly symmetrically, and no longer does cookery mean how to cook a rice pudding exactly scientifically, even if nobody likes it that way. No, the post-1951 schoolgirls are going to learn something far more real and useful, though it may be less tangible. They are going to learn what a home should really be like, how to make it like that, how to run it properly, how to keep its occupants well-fed and happy and, in general, how to create the atmosphere of a real home...

The kitchen shelves contained ample evidence of the practicality of their work, for I noticed jam, bottled fruit, pickles and chutney, and a bucket of pickled eggs under the sink, whose isinglass had made a nasty white stain where it had been spilled, even as mine does.

Yes, it's a real down-to-earth job, this housecraft, so much more practical than the domestic science it is to supersede.
Press Report on College Opening 26.9.1950. ESRO AMS6407/5

But what Seaford possesses in greater numbers than probably any other seaside place is schools, starting from what was the Ladies' College, now TRAINING COLLEGE, the most dignified building in the town. It was a private house, perhaps of c.1800, seven bays, two storeys, balustraded and stuccoed with a columnar porch and has since been extended much at the back. And then there are plenty of private schools, mostly of Edwardian or slightly later date, clean and cheerful-looking.
Ian Nairn and Nikolaus Pevsner, *Sussex, The Buildings of England*, 1965

Top hats were part of the uniform of the boys at Hilltop Court and their efforts to maintain their dignity, and headgear, walking in crocodile along the sea front on windy days, was one of the sights of Seaford. Crocodiles of school children were a familiar sight in the 1920s and 1930s and special road signs at each end of Sutton Avenue warned motorists of their presence. An old girl of the Downs School, now the Leisure Centre, was Fanny Craddock, one of television's first cookery experts; actor Nigel Davenport made his stage debut when a pupil at St Peter's School and another St Peter's boy grew up to be Colonel H Jones, VC, the Falklands war hero.
John Odam, *The Seaford Story 1000–2000 AD*

During the war most Seaford schools were evacuated and were requisitioned by the military. One of these was the Downs School (now the Downs Leisure Centre).

It was evacuated to St Ives in Cornwall. All the furniture and equipment was stored in a nearby house called Bydown, a road of the same name is now on this site. On August 9, 1942 this building received a direct hit from a German bomb during one of the biggest raids on Seaford. The headmistress Vera Pitt salvaged many items and as the weather was good, she was able to lay them all out for several hundred yards in the middle of Sutton Drove...

The school buildings were later used as the Headquarters of a Canadian Division, but when the school ended their tenure in Cornwall in July 1945, the Army remained at The Downs. This meant that the equipment from Cornwall, which had returned to Seaford by train, had to be temporarily stored in the gymnasium. Miss Pitt took on the Army and managed to persuade them that the remaining soldiers should be moved out into nearby Nissan huts.

A huge clean up operation took place – many floors and staircases had to be replaced as hob-nail boots had caused considerably more damage than the girls' felt 'house slippers'. The music room had been used by the Army to store hundreds of chamber pots and these all had to be moved out before music lessons could recommence...
175 Years, Sussex Express and County Herald Anniversary Edition 10.2.2012

At King's Mead School, Belgrave Road, two royal princes – both in their early teens – were among the pupils. Crown Prince Vajira-longkorn of Thailand was visited on more than one occasion by his parents and three sisters, while Prince Ronnie of Buganda had an unexpected call from his father the Kabaka, not long escaped from his homeland following a coup headed by rebel colonel Idi Amin.

Patricia Berry, *Seaford Memories 1950–1999*

The elderly and frail King George V [with Queen Mary] visited King's Mead School in May 1935 to visit Peter Beck, their Godson and one of the masters. When they arrived most of the boys were away on a scouting expedition, but they were hastily recalled to meet the royal guests. While waiting The Queen fed the ducks and signed the visitors' book.

SMA (Schools)

We should like to let all Old Boys know that King's Mead still stands undamaged where it did. The Mother Superior of the Convent, which is now in residence there, mildly deprecates the habit of Hurricane pilots, who fly as furiously as Jehu along the front of the building at dormitory level. She thinks that they must be Old Boys trying to catch a glimpse of the beds in which they slept in days of yore.

King's Mead Terminal Letters, Summer Term 1941 SMA (Schools) [the school was evacuated to Bideford, Devon during the war]

The School buildings stand in the best part of Seaford, one mile outside the town, near the Downs and Sea, and surrounded by private playing fields of about 12 acres. The drains and sanitary arrangements have been pronounced in perfect order by the Surveyor of the Seaford Urban District Council, and are thoroughly tested from time to time. The air of Seaford is strongly recommended by the medical profession, and in recent years Seaford has held the record for sunshine in all England.

…Great attention is paid to health, diet and manners. Fifth form boys do no work in the School after 5 o'clock, and a great deal of time is spent in the open air. When going to bed, and before and after meal-times, they are under the especial supervision of the matrons... The Classes are small, and lessons are of short duration. Boys receive much individual help and a good grounding is considered to be of the first importance. Arts and Crafts are a special feature of the time-table, e.g. Basketry, Rug-Making, Lino Cuts, Embroidery.

Chesterton School Prospectus, c 1955, SMA (Schools)

Though the road sign warning of 'Seven schools in the next half mile' of Sutton Avenue was still relevant, the description of Seaford as 'a windy place full of prep schools' hardly applied any more. Employable young people returned from the war with skills and knowledge not to be wasted on the domestic, odd job kinds of work which had kept so many schools ticking over in the 1930s. The 'almost continuous green belt of playing fields' surrounding the town, as described in 1937, was now being eyed by developers as ideal for housing expansion...

In spite of rumours in the 1960s that HRH Prince Charles might become a pupil there, St Peter's School, founded in Alfriston Road in 1904, suffered like so many others in the area from the changing approaches to education, and to boarding schools in particular. In 1983, shortly after one of its most distinguished former pupils, Colonel 'H' Jones, was posthumously awarded the Victoria Cross for his actions at the battle of Goose Green in the Falklands War, St Peter's closed.

Patricia Berry, *Seaford Memories 1950–1999*

Adult education provision at Seaford Head Community College will cease this year after it was found the centre there was not financially viable... The college has delivered courses to hundreds of adults in the local community under a franchise agreement with Sussex Downs, including courses for people with learning disabilities. Following a review by East Sussex County Council of the demand for adult education and the costs of the service it has been decided the current model cannot continue ... Seaford MP Norman Baker said, 'It's very sad indeed that this is going and I question if it is really necessary. How can it be that other towns with a smaller population can sustain such facilities including a sixth form facility and Seaford apparently can't? Seaford has been short-changed yet again.'

Seaford Gazette, 3.3.2010

Churches

St Leonard's Church

Things in and about it seem to have been in a rather dilapidated condition in AD 1724, according to the following answers in substance given at Bishop Bower's visitation that year: 'The church wants beautifying, and has some dangerous cracks and other defects in the outside walls; the Bible imperfect, and the common prayer book bad; two pewter flaggons, one silver cup with cover... No poor box; five bells new cast; no chancel; no mansion house nor any sort of building belonging to the vicarage. Seventy families; no Papists; three presbyterians in the parish. Divine service and sermon every Lord's day; number of communicants twenty or thirty.'

Descriptive Guide to Seaford, Newhaven and Vicinity, 189?

Church St, Seaford.

In 1778, in digging up the foundations of the old chancel, two coffin stones were discovered with handsome crosses carved upon them, a third was found close to the outer wall. The cist which the latter covered, contained sixteen skulls.

TW Horsfield, *History of Sussex*, 1835

There was nothing the Victorians liked more than to get their hands on an old Saxon or Norman church and modernise it. In 1862 they set about St Leonards, removing the external staircase which led to an upper gallery, installing gas lighting, additional seating and memorial windows commemorating local worthies...

John Odham, *Bygone Seaford*

In 1922 a war memorial was unveiled in the north-east chapel. It is made of white Sicilian marble framed in cream stone from a quarry in Somerset and lists the names of 93 local men who were killed in the war. The north-eastern annex has the feel of a military chapel, especially after the beautiful window to Maurice Galloway was installed. This shows a young soldier sleeping under a crucifix whilst in the background the French town of Givenchy burns. Givenchy was the place where teenage Private Galloway was killed.

Kevin Gordon, *St Leonard's & St Luke's Churches, Seaford, Magazine,* Mar/Apr 2011

The Non Conformist Chapel [now a community hall]

The memorial stone was laid by Mrs Crook, of Telsemaure House, on the 7th of December, 1877, and the opening services took place December 11th 1878. The interior arrangements of the building not only present an effective appearance, but also make it one of the most comfortable places of worship in the county. The warming is accomplished by 'Grundy's Patent Heating Apparatus', by means of which a most agreeable temperature is easily maintained, even in the coldest weather. At the rear are two schoolrooms, one for infants and the other for the general school. The latter is well fitted up, and is connected with the Chapel by sliding partitions, by the removal of which greatly increased accommodation may be given to the congregation – an arrangement of great advantage in the summer time... Cost of the building about £2,000.

W Banks, *Seaford: Past and Present. Handbook and Visitors' Guide*, 1892.

In a handsome lancet style, but with a turret so funny and so daring that it can only be High Victorian. It develops out of two angle-buttresses and is very thin.

Ian Nairn and Nikolaus Pevsner, *Sussex, The Buildings of England*, 1965

While sitting in the Congregational Church on Sunday November 5th 1899 he [Walter Nokes] received what he called a 'forcible impression' that he should start a Baptist cause in Seaford. Being a man of prompt action, he went home, and immediately consulted the current issue of 'The Christian', and found the name of an evangelist, Mr W Skinner of London, who sought an engagement. Mr Skinner arrived six days later and was engaged by Mr Nokes until the end of the year. He was to receive thirty shillings per week and the use of a furnished house, named 'The Lawns'. This was a beautiful house, with large lawns, where peacocks displayed their plumage.

Mr Nokes owned two shops at the corner of High Street and Church Street. These were providentially empty at the time, so he set men to work to pull down the partitioning walls. The resulting large room was decorated, gas laid on, and sixty chairs hired. Hand-bills were printed and distributed, notices put in the local press, and exactly two weeks after he received his 'forcible impression' the first services were held.

Seaford Baptist Church, 1899 to 1973

PEOPLE

Seaford Visitors and Residents

Saint Lewinna

A paper in the first volume of the 'Sussex Archaeological Collections' embodies a quaint story of a certain monk, Balger, of the priory of Bergue St Winox, whose vessel having been forced by stress of weather into Seaford Harbour, he contrived to rifle the neighbouring monastery of St Andrew of the bones of St Lewuina, one of the early Sussex apostles. The chronicler enthusiastically and antithetically extols him as 'fidelis fur et latro bonus' – a faithful rogue and an honest thief!
Black's 1861 Guide to Sussex

'We have no acts of the holy Virgin and Martyr, St Lewinna, nor any account of the honour rendered to her before the year 1058. At that time her sacred remains reposed in the Abbey Church of St Andrew, in or near Seaford, in Sussex, and was translated with great solemnity to the Church of St Winnoc at Berg, in Flanders. Eye witnesses have left on record that the progress of the holy relics was accompanied with a succession of innumerable miracles in the towns and villages through which they passed.'
LE Whatmore, *St Lewinna: East Sussex Martyr*

King John

King John, in one of his hurried journeys through the south of England, passed through this town, arriving on Monday, 23rd May 1216, and taking his leave the following day. He was en route from Canterbury to Winchester.
MA Lower, *Memorials of Seaford*, 1854

Thomas Elphick

Testimony signed by 18 inhabitants of Seaford as to the integrity of Thomas Elphicke, sen., jurat of Seaford, in purchasing the Common or Salts on behalf of the town [c 1595]

WHEREAS it is of late given forth in speeches by some malicious and envious persons: And that not onlie to some gentlemen of good worshippe and callinge, but also to Divers others that are of credit. That Thomas Elphicke the elder of Seaforde within the countie of Sussex Juratt. Shoulde have bought and purchased the common or salts of Seaforde unto his own proper Use his heirs and successors, by which meanes hee should have injured and greatlie oppressed the poore of the same towne to their great hinderaunce and undoinge Soe it is that we the Freemen and Commoners of the saide Towne heareinge and understandinge that this our Neighboure should be thus falslye and Unjustlie abused and the rather knowinge that both in regarde of his conscience towards god, and of his kindnesse and mercye towards the poore (as experience daylie sheweth) he never ment or intended any such wicked Acte, Doe thinke it meete and convenient as well for the avoidinge of all slaunders unjustlie objected against him, as also for the discharging of our consciences who have manye yeares knowne the good and honest disposition of his life To make knowne to as manye as are desirous to knowe the truith of this matter and allso to declare his honest and charitable meaninge in purchasinge of the same...
ESRO SEA/362

William Coombs [18th century miller at Blatchington]

It was said that William once swore that if something he had said proved to be untrue he would never set foot in his mill again. He was as good as his word. When he was proved to be wrong, he never again entered his mill. Instead he oversaw the work from the top of the mill steps, outside the mill door.

More eccentric still was his habit of not only painting his horse but painting it different colours. One week he would be seen riding down Blatchington Hill on a yellow horse, the next on a green horse. He even coloured his horse for visits to Lewes, where he might be seen on a horse of yellow, green or blue.

Rodney Castleden, *On Blatchington Hill, History of a Downland Village*

William Catt [owner of Tide Mills]

His faithful wife died in 1823 leaving him the responsible legacy of eleven children – the youngest being not an hour old. This bereavement seemed to stimulate him to renewed exertion and to extraordinary regard for little savings. He would always stop to pick up a nail or any scrap of old iron that lay in the road, and in the repeated enlargements and construction of his mills he was his own architect and surveyor; he was always pleased with the acquisition of a bit of wreck timber, any old materials from Blatchington barracks, or from the dismantled mansion of Bishopston Place, formerly the seat of the Duke of Newcastle. Yet he was ever bountiful as a host, liberal to his neighbours, and charitable to his dependents and the deserving poor.

MA Lower, *The Worthies of Sussex*, 1865

1817

Flour 2/11d a galon

25 June 1817

God grant it may soon fall

And Cat may fall with it

Is my wish

[Unsigned inscription on a plastered gable wall between numbers 2 and 3 Southover High Street, Lewes, in protest at the exorbitant cost of Tide Mills flour.]
Sussex Notes and Queries, SAS Vol XIV, 1957

The Duke of Wellington

Visit of the Duke of Wellington to Eastbourne and Seaford – On Friday last, the curiosity of the good people of Eastbourne was in no slight degree excited by the rumour that the Duke of Wellington had passed through the town on his way to Seaford. The report proved true, and it ultimately appeared that his Grace had passed the night at Seaford, and next morning, after an early walk before breakfast had returned to Eastbourne... It is almost needless to add that this

visit has given rise to numberless speculations as to its immediate object. The Harbour of Refuge, and the defence of the coast, afford ready subjects for such speculations.
Sussex Weekly Advertiser, 1845
[Reputedly, the Duke stayed at the New Inn which thereafter changed its name to The Wellington.]

The Bird Man of Blatchington

[1846] 9th December – headachy – sawed a little wood, not much better - walked to the Tide Mill Pond and watched men drawing a seine [fishing net] in the sluice hole. A scoter (black duck) was sitting on the shingle - shot at him. The dog jumped and caught part of the shot – he tumbled into the water and I was horribly frightened...

[1848] 5th May. Walked to the Tide Mill to settle my bill. Saw eight or ten Stone-Curlews opposite the Buckle Bank. They flew along the water's edge to the eastward.

How cunning the Ring-Dotterel are in drawing a dog or man away from their eggs.

I forget whether I mentioned that a Nightingale sang last Sunday and some evenings before. I have not heard it since.

[1861] 19th April. Saw a beautiful Hoopoe hopping about on the Seaford side of the Pond, after a while it flew across the Pond to the Sutton Drove about ninety yards, after a little while I followed it, and it had run onto a little hillock where it stood raising and depressing its crest and looking very graceful and beautiful in the full sun, and right against the sky...

[1867] 18th May. Took a walk under Seaford cliff. Saw seven Bar-tailed Godwits, the males having the reddish chestnut breast of the summer plumage. They alighted on the edge of the receding tide, and seemed greatly to enjoy bathing, and letting the waves wash over them. They were very tame, permitting me to walk quietly up within half gunshot on the open beach without cover of any sort.
Notes on Sussex Ornithology, the diaries of Robert Nathaniel Dennis

Alfred Lord Tennyson

November 27th 1852

My dear Colquhoun

Many thanks for your note received here where myself, wife and babe have been for some weeks and shall be till Christmas... I am distressed to hear of your 'maiden' fit of gout tho' perhaps I ought rather to be glad. Doctors have more than once told me that a fit of gout would be the making of me... I trust, my dear fellow, that you will arise from your couch of torment a stronger man – nay, that ere this you are already risen for I see your date is 22 and today is 27. I am very glad too that you like my Civic Ode; it was expected of me so I wrote it. I intend to put in another passage or two if it gets another edition. Moxon gave me £200 for the first 10,000 copies which was handsome, I think.

Now goodbye and believe me

      Dear Colquhoun

         Ever Yours

           A Tennyson

Seaford House, Seaford, Sussex. November 27.

Best regards from my wife. The bairn is very stout and healthy.

JF Tattersall, *Tennyson at Seaford*, SCM Vol 3, 1929

It has been said hundreds of times that Tennyson wrote his Ode [to Wellington] at Seaford, but all he can have done to it here is to revise it, for it was written by the Thames and not by the sea. The house in which the poet used to stay has gone, but the garden is still on the hill, crowned with glorious cedars by which Tennyson would stand and look out at the sea.

Arthur Mee, *Sussex*, 1937

General Gordon

Visitors to Seaford will have, however, an interesting as well as a touching association with this place, when they learn that the late General Gordon often when a boy came on visits to his aunt, the wife of Captain Wallinger, who then occupied the 'Crouch House' which stands at the north-east corner of the Crouch.

Descriptive Guide to Seaford, Newhaven and Vicinity, 189?

Thomas Crook was born in London in 1814. He married Sarah and they had several children, the oldest son being Lewis born in 1839. When Thomas moved to Seaford his wife became involved with helping the local people. She dispensed soup during cold days from a room in Dane Road and also bought meat and coal for the poor to see them through the cold winter months. She would keep a stock of blankets at Telsemaure which she would distribute each October, carefully packed in parcels to ensure that there was at least one blanket for each member of the family...

Thomas died in Eastbourne in 1873 but Sarah kept on her philanthropic work, being affectionately known as the 'Queen of Seaford'...

...Like his mother, Lewis Crook also became a beloved Seaford character. He could often be seen in town on his horse, Philosopher – sometimes with a tame raven called Jack perched on his shoulder.

...He ensured that his family observed Sabbath not only by attending church three times every Sunday but also ensuring that they did not ride a bicycle or take out a boat.

On other days, however, boating was definitely allowed. Lewis taught all his children to swim, sometimes by tipping them into the cold waters of Seaford Bay from his dinghy, the Cockleshell. On some sunny days the whole family would take a fleet of rowing boats around Seaford Head to picnic on the shore at Cuckmere Haven.

Sarah Crook died in 1901 at the grand old age of 93 years. The rest of the family stayed in Seaford until just before the Great War when they moved to Wallington in Surrey.

Kevin Gordon, *From a Seaford Album*, Sussex Express, 22 June 2007

Horace Plowman [future son-in-law of Lewis Crook]

Lochnagar, Bycullah Park, Enfield, February 2nd 1907
Dear Major and Mrs Crook
... As you know, Gertie and I have had a long, long wait for one another – a good deal longer than we were expecting this time a year ago – but now we are hoping that with your approval we shall be able to be married about the middle of next May. We shall have

between £200 and £250 a year, and I think if we are careful that ought to be enough for us to make both ends meet, especially as it may be increased at any time …

Hoping to hear that there will be no difficulty about next May, provided that our expectations are realised, I am

Yours affectionately

Horace

SMA (P) [Horace and Gertie were eventually married in July 1907]

Dr William Tyler-Smith

Once Seaford was linked to the outside world by rail Dr Tyler-Smith, who as it happened, owned almost all the land over which the line passed, and had built the Terminus Hotel opposite the station for the convenience of travellers, set about doing for the town what Dr Russell had done for Brighton and Dr Charles Lees Prince for Crowborough – advertising its health giving properties. He also converted the bath house and reading room on the beach into Assembly Rooms, a facility considered essential for English spa towns of the period, and had another hotel, the Bay, under construction at the time of his death in 1873.

John Odam, *The Seaford Story, 1000–2000 AD*

Robert Lambe

The last squire of Blatchington was Robert Lambe. His late nineteenth century term as Blatchington's major landowner saw enormous changes, many of them precipitated by the ambitious scale of his financial dealings. It was in the fall-out from his huge debts that land in and round Blatchington was sold off for building, and the character of the village was changed for ever.

Rodney Castleden, *On Blatchington Hill, History of a Downland Village*

It is stated that Mr Lambe is about to repair the road from Blatch-ington to Firle Beacon, and so make it an easy drive to that pictur-esque spot. The view from the height on a clear day is well worthy a visit, while the drive is one of the most beautiful. This should prove a great attraction to the town and be the means of inducing many visitors to come among us. The thanks of all will be heartily accorded to Mr Lambe for kindly undertaking this much-needed improvement.

SMA (TRA2)1889

Rosalie Harvey and the Lepers

She was born just after the middle of the 19th century at Seaford, daughter of the vicar here.

From her earliest girlhood she dreamed of caring for unhappy beings and something in the stories of the Far East caught her imagination. When she was 28 she managed to go out for the Zenana Medical Mission to Poona, and a little later moved on to Nasik where she worked all the rest of her life. Not once could she be persuaded to leave her work for a little visit to her family...

But when this brave woman looked back on her life she knew that her work among the lepers was her great achievement. During years of plague and famine she had worked in a relief camp and met such cases of leprosy that she felt as if nothing mattered but caring for such sufferers. She begged a little money, built an iron shelter, put 35 lepers into it, and remained in charge to the end.

Arthur Mee, *Sussex*, 1937

James Hurdis [poet]

The following characteristics of Hurdis are given in his sister's account. 'He was tall, but well-proportioned: his countenance serene and lively: of a fair complexion with flaxen hair. His disposition was meek, affectionate, benevolent, and cheerful; yet occasionally irritable and impatient. With his intimate friends he was affable, polite, and familiar; but in mixed company generally reserved... His piety was fervent and unaffected.' His portrait engraved by his eldest son from a drawing by Sharples gives to his face a remarkably delicate and almost feminine character. His epitaph at Bishopston was written by his friend Hayley.

MA Lower, *The Worthies of Sussex*, 1865

On a certain Sunday I set forth to Seaford on my way to make a pilgrimage to the tomb of James Hurdis, a forgotten Sussex poet, now lying in Bishopstone Church. Bishopstone is by Seaford and Newhaven; and in its charming church I found a tablet to Hurdis, friend of Cowper and poet of the school of Crabbe...

When I had paid my reverence to the name of the Sussex poet, I came out of the church and strode about the deep-bosomed Downs, thinking of the man who lay in its tiny chancel, forgotten by the world. I thought how easy it is for the memory of a man, who has made a mark in his day, to die; and I told myself that it was absurd for any man to work for fame, and that the only true reward of labour is the satisfaction that comes from the work itself.

Arthur Beckett, *The Spirit of the Downs*, 1949

George Meredith [novelist]

Through Fitzgerald it was that I was brought into contact with Meredith, Burnard and others, and enjoyed delightful times together at Seaford, then quite an unknown little place, a sort of village of the dead...

Henry Mayers Hyndman, *The Record of an Adventurous Life*, 1911

But Meredith's visit to Seaford was not a conventional seaside holiday. He was 28 and still a young, unknown writer; he felt that he had failed to make his mark as a poet. His poems had been published and favourably reviewed; some critics commented on his kinship with Keats, though he did not have Keats's high abilities. He was turning to prose in the hope that he might make his way as a novelist instead. While at Seaford he wrote part of *The Ordeal of Richard Feverel*, which would be his first full-length novel. He had brought his wife, Mary Ellen Nicolls, and their three-year-old son Arthur to live for a few months in Seaford because he had found lodgings on the seafront where they could live very cheaply. He was having difficulty in supporting his family and his marriage was in a state of collapse. One of his friends was seducing her and trying to persuade her to go off with him instead. She was on the point of leaving Meredith, and he was in despair over it.

Rodney Castleden, *On Blatchington Hill, History of a Downland Village*

Field Marshal, lst Earl Kitchener

A vivid memory of the year 1915 was the historic occasion when Lord Kitchener drove up the school drive to review the troops. They were encamped all around the field, just behind where Little St Peter's is now. He mounted a horse just in front of the school, and when the asscmbled boys gave three high-pitched cheers, the horse reared up and nearly threw the great man. I remember quite well that, contrary to all the photographs and posters of Lord Kitchener at that time, his hair and moustache were not black but almost white.

St Peter's School [Seaford] *Magazine,* Vol III 1974, SMA (Schools)

Margaret Rutherford

Margaret was the daughter of William Benn and Florence Rutherford but shortly before her birth in 1892 her father murdered her grand-father so she took her mother's maiden name. She was sent to Seaford to attend Ravens Croft School where she developed an interest in music and theatre.

In 1925 Margaret was accepted as a student at the Old Vic Theatre where she appeared in several roles. She appeared on stage in The Importance of Being Earnest, Blithe Spirit and The Happiest Days of Your Life and later played the same roles when they were made into feature films.

Margaret Rutherford appeared as Agatha Christie's Miss Marple in several films and won an Oscar for her role in the 1963 film The VIPs.

Margaret Rutherford was made a Dame in 1967 and died in 1972.

Kevin Gordon, *Seaford Schools,* 2002, SMA

Peter White (Town Crier)

THE LOUDEST man in Seaford has finally got dressed. Town crier, Peter White unveiled his new uniform at the Seaford Fun Day on Saturday. The uniform, the first authentic one to be worn by a Seaford crier in 96 years, was made possible thanks to the fund raising of the local community. Collecting jars were placed in local shops, funding organiser Val Rogers went on a sponsored slim,

Seaford, Newhaven and Peacehaven Lions organised a sponsored swim and donations from individuals and Lewes District Council all enabled Peter to show off his new togs.

Peter says he has scoured top outfitters in his quest for accuracy, from the hat supplied by Patey of London to the boots supplied by Jones, of Eastbourne. He added, 'It has been a long haul to raise the money, research the authentic design and to find a firm willing and able to make the uniform. I trust people will appreciate the historically accurate style.'

Seaford Gazette, 3.9.1997

Don Partridge

Tributes have been paid to well-known busker and former Seaford resident Don Partridge, who toured the world to bring music to the ears of thousands of people... During his colourful life he met many characters and had several hits in the charts. His love of music started from a young age and he was influenced by his family – his father played the guitar and his uncle played the piano and accordion. Don, who had an interest in Blues and Folk, began busking in his late teens. In 1967 he was discovered by Don Paul from Essex Music and he went on to have several hits, most notably Rosie which got to number four in the charts, Blue Eyes and Breakfast on Pluto got to number three and 30 respectively... Richard Durrant, of Long-Man Records, who recorded The Highwayman – Don's last ever studio album – with the late busker paid tribute to his friend. He said, 'He was an absolutely amazing performer. I totally respect what he did, he was a one-off.'

Seaford Gazette, 29.9.2010

Clergy

John Hubbersty, Curate of Seaford and Bishopstone 1755-1758

Dear Bro,
I have been in hopes of an Answer from you ever since my last letter, but as I have not been so happy as to receive one, I am obliged once more to repeat my Solicitations. I was so lucky as to gain credit for

what I wanted against the Bishop of Durham's and Thomas Gage's coming into the Country, but as the Lewes Tradesmen have lately been bit by some of my Profession, they are apt to make a noise if similar debts come to any long standing; it's true I have not been called on yet, and had rather be enabled to pay before I am asked. I have hitherto maintained a fair character among all ranks? But that I am sure to forfeit, if I am found unable to answer my necessary Debts. I cannot accuse myself of having spent anything, since I came to Seaford, in an idle extravagant manner; I have had but bare necessaries, and these my Curacy will scarcely furnish. The Truth is, it is impossible to live upon £35 [per annum?] in such a dear country as this, and I hope 5 or 6 guineas in two years cannot put you to any great inconvenience; besides I think I may reasonably expect to be in a better situation ere long...

    I desire my love to Sister and am

Dear Bro:

your most affectionate Bro:

Seaford 29 Augt 1757   J Hubbersty

PS The Duke of Newcastle did not come down at Whitsuntide as was expected but came down to Lewes Races. He was at Bishopstone (which is one of the Parishes I supply) yesterday fortnight, and gave me of his usual entertainment. We were in all about 950 people that dined with him. A turtle was dressed which weighed 350 lb.

ESRO AMS 6126

Carnegie soon resigned Bishopstone, and John Harison was appointed Vicar. John Harison lived at Sutton, two miles from his church. One Sunday morning, on reaching Bishopstone Church, he found a strange clergyman in the reading-desk, already commencing the service. He quietly went into a pew and let the stranger go on. At the conclusion of the service he spoke to the strange clergyman, and then found out that the cleric, who was staying at Seaford, had undertaken to take the service at Blatchington, and had mistaken the church.

    Meanwhile a congregation had been waiting in Blatchington Church, and did not know what to think. After a long waiting, Mr Catt, the churchwarden, stood up in his seat and read the prayers.

The matter was referred to the Bishop; but as Mr Catt evidently meant well, he merely received a kind letter from the Bishop, pointing out to him that he did wrong and must not do the like again.

...The Rev Joseph Kahn, Vicar of Bishopstone (in later years) was also a converted Jew. The history of his conversion was as follows: To escape the conscription he was fleeing his country and was waiting at a seaport in Holland when he was spoken to by a stranger, who recognised him as a Jew and spoke to him of Christ. The stranger stated that he himself was a Jew by birth, but a convert to Christianity, and urged Kahn to become one too. They embarked together in a small sailing vessel, hoping to reach England in safety. During the passage they were nearly lost in a storm. While in the midst of the storm his fellow Jew increased his urgency, and exacted from Kahn a promise that if they escaped safe to land he would read the New Testament and study the subject. After a fearful passage the vessel arrived at an English port. Mr Kahn was thus led to study Christianity, and ultimately to take Orders in our Church.

...The Vicar of Seaford, Carnegie, who retained his buoyancy of spirits to the end, on one occasion, in order to arouse Mr Bedford, expressed himself in a higher church tone than he probably otherwise would have done. Whereupon Mr Bedford exclaimed, 'Really, Mr Carnegie, one would think that you were a Catholic priest!' 'I trust I am,' Mr Carnegie simply replied.

Rev Edward Boys Ellman, *Recollections of a Country Parson* 1925

Politicians

The Pelhams

In most country districts politics were controlled by the local landed gentry. Although Seaford, Blatchington and Sutton had families which might have formed a squirearchy, they were totally over-shadowed in the 18th century by the powerful Pelham family which had vast estates in various counties including property at Laughton, a few miles north of Seaford. As Seaford was one of what came to be known as the 'rotten boroughs', where a handful of electors voted for two members of parliament, it was a tempting political prize and the Pelhams kept Bishopstone Place as a base from which to direct and control the voters of Seaford, using the local gentry and placemen (sinecure holders) as their agents.

John Odam, *Bygone Seaford*

Robert Jones

'Seaford 24th June 1775

To those merciless maneaters who would enslave the present age and bind their children with fetters, he will secure and insure to the residents and inhabitants if they are united and firm to each other, all their privileges granted by their charter, to them and their heirs for ever, in defence of all the tools of oppression and on their creatures. He hopes and trusts you have courage and fortitude and unanimity as himself till they establish all their just rights, liberties and privileges and then they will thereafter be called, the Honest and Independent Residents and Inhabitants of Seaford.

Robert Jones.'

Joan A Astell, *To the Independent Electors of Seaford, 1768–1786*

Robert Jones was not a Seafordian and mercifully for the town he stayed not long in it. The first notice we have of his arrival comes in an advertisement in a local paper of 19th October 1772 when he advertises for journeymen shoemakers. He appears to have set up something of a factory here because in the second advertisement he is asking for quite a large number of men, and by April 1773 he is asking for as many as 20 men. In the light of Mr Jones' future conduct it may be well to wonder if the employment of so many men was some effort to retain them in his interest.

7th March 1744 sees Mr Jones in print as the saviour of Seaford. Then commenced a wild career and finally culminated in a fine of £10 and two months in prison resulting from his behaviour in the town hall in 1776. After this he left, never to be heard of again. Why he ever came here in the first instance has remained a mystery and the only conclusion that can be placed upon it is that he was one of these eccentric people whom politics throw up every now and then.

Joan A Astell, *Ibid*

Thomas Hinton Birley Oldfield
...His stay in Seaford was comparatively short but like Mr Jones it was not without event, he instigated a riot at the town hall in 1789 and he and his wife were both physically assaulted in their own home by political agents, he arranged a duel between two leading men of the town, and like his enemy Mr Harben went bankrupt. By 1790 Mr Oldfield and his family had disappeared from the Seaford scene and he is last heard of languishing in the Fleet debtors' prison.
Joan A Astell, *Ibid*

In the *Journals of the House of Commons* of February 4 1641 is the entry: 'Resolved that the town of Seaford, having sent burgesses to Parliament in former times... should be restored to its ancient privilege of sending burgesses.'

And send burgesses it did – among them William Pitt the Elder, later Lord Chatham, one of the greatest of English statesmen; Philip Yorke, a future Lord Chancellor; and George Canning, for the election of whom in 1826 one of Seaford's representatives, Major Augustus Frederick Ellis of the 60th Regiment of Infantry, was 'persuaded to accept the stewardship of the manor of East Hendred', one of the Chiltern Hundreds, and so vacate his Parliamentary seat. He soon regained it, for a few months after succeeding Lord Liverpool as prime minister in 1827 George Canning died.
John Odam, *The Seaford Story 1000–2000 AD*

The day of the funeral [George Canning] was a solemn one at Seaford. The whole of the shops were closed, and blinds of private houses drawn, and the bells tolled throughout the day.
W Banks, *Seaford: Past and Present* 1892

Mr [Norman] Baker will go to his grave with the distinction of having felled Peter Mandelson... He plunged the stake through Mr Mandelson's heart by a technique no more fearsome than the patient and persistent use of the parliamentary question.
The Spectator: Inquisitor of the Year, 18th Annual Parliamentarian of the Year Awards 16th February 2002

DISASTERS AND INCLEMENT WEATHER

...the town was struck by a series of disasters in the 14th century. Appointed as a limb of the Cinque Ports as early as 1229, Seaford supplied ships and men for the war effort. But frequent French pirate attacks, the Black Death and regular floodings, led remaining inhabitants to abandon the town. Lord Poynings, the town's Patron, planned a new town on the lower slopes of Seaford Head, to the east of the present narrow road leading to the car park on the Head. This site seems to have been only partially occupied, perhaps because Seafordians realised that acceptance of this 'new town' meant abandonment of the harbour, of riverside quays and warehouses, and of their maritime occupations. It seems that Lord Poynings, as others before him, had realised that, for Seaford as a Port, the writing was on the wall.

Edna and Mac McCarthy, *Sussex River, Seaford to Newhaven*
[Poynings Town was excavated in 2010 and no sign of the village was found]

Floods

29th November 1824

From Seaford we have most dreadful accounts. A large portion of the town under water, two hay-stacks washed away, buildings flooded, one man had his leg broke by falling off of a wall. The damage done is estimated at £2,000.

At Bishopstone the Tide Mill was for a considerable time thought to be in great danger but it outstood the violence of the wind and overflowing of the tide which was so excessive and so much so that a lighter that had just discharged her cargo of coals was forced from her moorings and driven by the flood a good part of a mile (not long before dry land) towards Bishopstone church and its passage forced down some of the walls on the premises of the Earl of Chichester.

At Bletchington the tide overflowed the fishpond of J King and the salt water destroyed all his carp. The inhabitants of Seaford were for some hours in the utmost consternation, the sea with resistless fury having swept away the full or bar of the beach in front of the town presently flowed into the streets some of which were completely inundated, while the inhabitants of some of the houses were up their middles in water and were only rescued from the perilous situation by the aid of boats which were brought to their assistance. Happily no lives were lost but the damage sustained in the town and neighbourhood is incalculable.
A letter from Alfriston. SMA (WEA)

There was a grand sight here just near noon at high water. The sea was coming right over the bank, the road was flooded and a beautiful cascade of water was falling over the road into the valley between the coastguard station and Blatchington Battery.
Sussex Weekly Advertiser, 28.10.1862. SMA (WEA1)

In the great storm about 11 years ago [1875], in which the town of Seaford was almost completely wrecked, the furniture of the houses was floated eight miles over the marsh to Lewes.
Coventry Patmore, *Hastings, Lewes, Rye and the Sussex Marshes*

...The inflow was the result in the first place of one stupendous wave, which carrying away the crown of the beach drove everything before it. So rapid was the rise of the water that in a short time those who had not left their houses were only able to do so by the use of boats. As a matter of precaution, tow-lines were fastened to the boats, so that the force of the current should not carry them out to sea. In about half-an-hour the water had risen nearly to the top of the lamp posts on the parade, the second floors of some of the houses being by this time flooded. The High Street for half way up was submerged, the water running into the letter box at the Post Office, which fortunately had been cleared in anticipation of such a result. Timbers from a recent wreck, which had been stranded on the beach, were carried a considerable distance up into the town, and formed a powerful ally in the work of destruction, being dashed with terrific force against the houses on the front, smashing doors and windows and making fearful breaches in the walls. From this time till noon, when the tide was at its highest, a scene of the greatest confusion and consternation was witnessed. Furniture of all descriptions was floating about in every direction...

There were several narrow escapes, and among others Mr Wood, butcher, of High Street, whose premises adjoin the quaint little Town Hall, had a rough time of it. About a quarter to twelve, when the tide was at its height, he waded out through the yard with the water breast high to his stables, with the view of rescuing his pony and cob. The pressure outwards was so great that he was unable to open the doors of the stable; he, therefore, with assistance, effected an entrance through the door of the loft above, and got down the ladder. His retriever had been confined there, and the poor animal was so glad to see its master that it jumped on to his shoulders and sent him under water. Recovering himself he forced open the stable door and got out the pony without much difficulty. With the cob, however, he had more trouble; a vehicle was floating about in the yard, and the shafts unfortunately being in the way, Mr Wood fell over them, and the cob being restive, rushed forward and kept him down in a very narrow space. However he managed to extricate himself and escaped with a severe ducking and some very unpleasant bruises.
Sussex Weekly Advertiser, 16th November 1875

...a haystack, which had been standing at Lyon's Place, was carried away by the tide and stranded at Chyngton, nearly half a mile distant, and on the top of it were a number of fowls who had taken refuge there, none the worse for their journey. At the old Assembly Rooms a billiards table was washed out of the billiards rooms and, curious to relate, was found three or four days later washed ashore at Cuckmere but very little damaged. In fact it was brought back, repaired, and used afterwards for some years...
WR Wynter, *Old Seaford,* 1922

17th November 1894. Brickyard belonging to Mr Funnell in the dip between Beach Cottages and Coastguard Station flooded as the water reached the kilns great clouds of steam were generated and watched by huge crowds – loss £400.
SMA (WEA)

Explosion

At 3.10 pm General Burgoyne gave the signal from the Martello Tower ... A moment afterwards and the batteries had fulfilled their task – a low rumbling was heard and an immense mass of cliff was observed bulging outwards and then gliding slowly down into the sea. In a few minutes after the cliff had fallen the crowd upon the beach rushed forward, but a second fall of chalk when they had gone half way, halted them momentarily. Ten ladies eagerly clambered up the mass of rough stones and one gentleman was observed to get his horse up on to the top of the fallen chalk.

The Illustrated London News, 28th September 1850.

[Unsuccessful attempt on 19th September to create a natural chalk groyne. Charles Dickens was reputedly a spectator]

Storms, Snow and Lightning

Extraordinary Fall of Hailstorms - On Sunday evening, March 31st, 1897, about 6.30, Seaford was visited by one of the most extraordinary storms ever seen in this country, accompanied by a fall of hailstones of the most abnormal size. All of the day the atmosphere was very oppressive, and suddenly, about 6.30 pm, huge masses of clouds appeared, coming up with tremendous speed from the north-west, accompanied by a curious cracking sound. There was very little wind at the time, and within a very few minutes hailstones of enormous size commenced to fall. The size of the stones (or they might be termed chunks of ice) can be easily estimated by the fact that nine of them (which the writer picked up in his garden) weighed just over three-quarters of a pound, some of them being the size of small oranges. The fall lasted only for seven minutes, but during that short time considerable damage was done to glass, fowls, etc in the town. In fact it was estimated that over 3,000 panes of glass were broken, mostly in greenhouses and the like... On being broken most of them showed a peculiar star shape in the centre...
SMA (WEA)

Only a fortunate combination of circumstances saved Seaford from the sea in 1987. Had the hurricane force winds which swept across southern England in the early hours of October 16th uprooting millions of trees, tearing roofs off houses, toppling church spires, overturning vehicles, and blowing down overhead power lines come six months earlier, the low lying part of the town would have been lost. What saved it was:

a) Southern Water's decision to go ahead with its sea defence plan.
b) The government not deferring to a later date approval and funding for the £9 million scheme, and
c) The contract going to the Dutch Zanen group of companies which did the work in half the time allowed.

John Odam, *The Seaford Story*

An 80-year-old woman had a miracle escape in her caravan home at The Buckle, Seaford. She insisted on staying in her caravan all night, despite pleas from park managers to come out. She appeared the next day, unharmed.

Sussex Express & County Herald, *Special Hurricane Issue,* 23.10.1987

Snow

The next day it tried to snow and thereafter arctic winds kept us indoors or made walks the only possible source of exercise. Snow came in earnest on Sunday, January 26th, and for the next five weeks rarely left us. After a season of such severity it is inevitable that everyone has a good snow story. In this area we felt very sorry for ourselves, but considering what happened in parts to the north, we escaped very lightly.

...Friday, February 7th, was Black Friday for the whole country. Our time table fortunately fits well with the fuel cuts...

King's Mead [Seaford] *Terminal Letters,* Easter Term 1947, SMA (Schools)

The snow has caused havoc across Sussex in the past week with Seaford being particularly badly hit. Several schools in the area were closed from last Wednesday and did not re-open until the beginning of this week and travelling into the town was problematic for many motorists with road closures in the area... Many motorists were unable to access Seaford and on Sunday a driver was stuck on the hill between Seaford and High and Over hill after the road between the

coastal town and Alfriston was closed to all traffic. Many bus and train services were also disrupted as temperatures plummeted to around -5C, leaving many employees unable to get to work. Despite the wide-spread disruption many children, who were off school for much of the week, made the most of the snow and headed to Seaford Head with sledges...
Seaford Gazette, 13.1.2010

Lightning

22nd May, 1809. At three o'clock on last Friday afternoon this town and neighbourhood were visited by a severe storm of thunder, lightning, hail and rain which continued with more or less violence until near seven in the evening when John Bouchert, a baker of Seaford on his return home from Newhaven in company with two other persons on foot was struck by lightning in front of Mr Catt's Tide Mill at Bishopstone and instantaneously killed. He was much scorched by the electric fire particularly about the face and head and some blood issued from one of his ears, his coat, waistcoat, breeches, stockings and shirt were literally torn to tatters and so dispersed that his body was left nearly naked. His hat and shoes were also much rent by the active power of the fluid. The string of his watch was cut asunder and the outer case of silver melted the enamel of which formed the face was stripped off and the brass or copper beneath left quite bare but otherwise without injury. Mr Catt and his servants witnessed the melancholy catastrophe and on going to the spot found the tattered parts of the clothes which did remain about the body on fire. ONE HUNDRED AND EIGHTY FIVE PIECES of scattered garments were collected together with a great number of the fragments. A very hard part of the footpath about a yard in length where the unfortunate man fell, the companions of the deceased were both knocked down and severely electrified that bleeding was deemed necessary and one was so seriously affected that he is not yet perfectly recovered.
SMA (WEA)

A Coastguardsman Killed by Lightning – A frightful accident has occurred to a coastguardsman named Dancer, it will be remembered a terrific storm was raging, and before the rain commenced the lightning and thunder were very heavy. About half past nine, Dancer had a conference with the Cuckmere coastguardsman at the signal-post on the cliff, to the east of Seaford. The next morning the poor fellow was found on the beach at the bottom of the cliff by Mr Bennett, chief boatswain at the Blatchington battery. His hat and stick were discovered at the top of the cliff, and at the spot the cliff is about 200 feet high. Police Constable Selmes was called before the deceased was touched, and on his arrival he examined the body. He found one arm broken, and one of his thighs was also broken, and the bone protruded for a considerable distance. He had also sustained a severe cut over the left eye, and he was very much cut and bruised about the body. His chest, too, seemed completely broken in. What makes the matter so peculiar is, that the man was lying about six yards from where he at first fell. He has left a mark in the beach where he had fallen, and he was found lying on his back with a handkerchief round his head, one arm lying across his face, and his legs crossed.

Lloyd's Weekly Newspaper 5.7.1863

The *Sussex Daily News* reports that during the storm of Monday last a curious incident occurred at Blatchington Battery. A soldier was sitting in his rooms, and a table knife that he had just been using lay beside him, when the lightning entered the apartment, struck the knife, cutting it completely in two, and throwing the pieces about the room, and being taken nearly up to the ceiling. The man was not hurt, but naturally very much frightened.

The Star, 16.6.1877

Accidents and Frights

11 July 1863, Sussex Express. Seaford – Fatal accident on the New Railway. On Thursday afternoon, 2nd, a labourer named Thomas Fox was accidentally killed on the railway in course of construction between this town and Newhaven. The deceased was driving a wagon laden with chalk drawn by one horse, and by some means fell under the wheel just as the wagon was about to discharge its contents down the embankment. He was instantaneously crushed to death.

The Revd Robert Nathaniel Dennis, *Diaries*

A boat belonging to Mr Catt brought on shore at Seaford, a few days ago, a fish of an extraordinary kind. Its fins resembled the arms and hand, with fingernails, of a human being, and it had two protuberances or sort of pockets on each breast, which were filled with small fish. When taken from the net it followed the fishermen round the boat, and in order to get rid of 'so ugly a customer' they procured weapons and despatched it forthwith – (*Brighton Gazette*)
Morning Post, 9.8.1833

It was only when the house fell hushed at 11 pm that Ivan heard a noise under his blanket-covered games table.

'Something black suddenly burst out and ran behind the curtains across the French doors,' he said. 'I could see its shape moving – it was about 3 ft high. Then a giant black head with green eyes came out of the side'...

He called the police and later had a visit from Derek Bilston, of Sussex Big Cat Watch, who confirmed from his description that their house guest had been a black panther – about the size of a Labrador with a long tail... Mr Bilston said: 'Their house is very close to open countryside at Seaford Head.' Now 4ins paw prints found outside the property are also being investigated.
Sussex Express and County Herald, 10.2.2012

A ROUGH SEA, SEAFORD. 12870.

EVENTS

Eating and Drinking

[1756] Mon 7 June. This day my brother having affixed to go to Brighthelmstone in order to bathe in the sea and from which I dissuaded him from doing, thinking he would get into bad company and get in liquor, but upon these conditions: that I would accompany him to some other part of the sea coast; so accordingly about 8 o'clock he and I set out from Hoathly on foot for Seaford where we arrived about 11.30. My brother and I went down to the sea, wherein he bathed and came back and dined at The Tree at Seaford on veal steaks (not deserving the name of cutlets); and for which dinner we paid 9d apiece, though I think as badly dressed as I ever saw a dinner, and nothing set at table but salt.

[1758] Tues 7 Mar. In the morn about 5 o'clock my brother and I set out on our intended journey. We arrived at Seaford about 8.20 where, after viewing the goods (which consisted of about 26 quarters of peas, 18 quarters groats [grain], 5230 lbs of Smyrna raisins, and 20 bags of hops – all very much damaged with sea-water) in company with Mr Geo. Beard, we then walked down to the sea-side. The sale begun about 11.20 when the peas was sold from 15s to 22s per quarter, and the groats nearly the same, the raisins from about 14s to 18s per cwt. But they having lost much of their goodness, neither Mr Beard or myself bought any.

[1762] Sun 1 Aug... There being only prayers at our church in the afternoon (and that more than we knew of till we came from church) Sam Jenner and I took a ride to Seaford where we took a walk by the seaside and took a view of the two forts newly erected there, one of which has 5 24-pounders mounted and the other 5 12-pounders. We drank tea at the sign of The Tree. Came home by Alfriston where we overtook on the road my servant and Tho. Durrant.

We came home about 11.10 – oh, could I say thoroughly sober. I think I am the most unfortunate fellow in the world, for only a few glasses of wine intoxicates my brains. I was not so far intoxicated today as to be guilty of any indiscretion, but still though we only took a ride with no other design than innocent inoffensive amusement, and with an intention of reaping the advantage of serious and improving conversation from each other, yet being guilty of this one folly, the whole of our journey must become contaminated, which otherwise could not have been more than a breach of an active obedience. Each of us spent today as follows: to tea 6d, wine 6d, beer 2d, horses 4d, a-coming home 7½d.

The Diary of Thomas Turner 1754–1765

The events causing the most excitement were, to use the language of the town, the 'lection balls,' and, of course, as there were two parties, there had to be two balls – the one at the Old Tree would be for the supporters of Ellis and Fitzgerald, and the other at the New Inn for the supporters of Lyon and Williams ...It mattered little whether one's partner in the 'merry dance' had a snuffy nose or fair skin, all footed it merrily; not any went short of the goods, and if by chance there should be more than was required, to avoid the trouble of sending the overplus down stairs, the novel mode of lowering the same out of the window was resorted to – friends below were at all times waiting to receive the same, whether it might be beef, pudding, cake, spirits or wine.

W Banks, *Seaford: Past and Present*, 1892

My own duty, as a rule, was to preside at the till, to supply the men with tickets of different values, according to the amount which they wished to spend, and, incidentally, also, often to give my solemn advice regarding the rival attractions of the refreshments provided on the counter. Sausage-rolls versus ham-pies, penny cakes and buns versus three-half-penny slices of superior cake, and other problems of like importance.

Agnes H Carter, *A Canteen in a Canadian Camp* (1917), SCM Vol 8, 1934

Visits

Shortly afterwards Mrs Radcliffe [18th century novelist] visited Alfriston from Seaford via the High and Over, 'over such a road as I never saw before; and travelling over such hills!' Two men helped the chaise down one of them but she was too frightened to ride on her return and chose to walk the greatest part of the way back to Seaford.
Peter Brandon, *The Discovery of Sussex*

Jeremiah Milles's tours in Sussex, 1743
... From hence I rode eight miles over the downs through a very pleasant country to Seaford, a poor miserable village situated on the sea shore, but as there is no port to it the fisherboats are drawn up upon the beach for security. Seaford is I think a member of the Cinque Port of Hastings. It sends two Barons to Parliament, for that is the name the representatives of the Cinque Ports bear.

About a mile to the east of Seaford is a hill called South Hill on which there is a camp but of what form I cannot exactly determine as I was not upon it.

From Seaford I went along the seaside for a mile, and then turning to the right passed by Bishopstone where the Duke of Newcastle has a small hunting seat which stands conveniently enough for that diversion, but otherwise its situation is disagreeable enough, being in a naked, open country where there is hardly a tree to be seen.
John Farrant, *Sussex Depicted*

June 22nd 1835. Wednesday. Drove to Eastbourne on a visit to my friend Mr Davies Gilbert. Called on Mr Harrison at Folkington, and inspected a fine collection of Roman Urns in his possession: they were dug up in a mound or barrow at Sutton near Seaford...
Gideon Mantell, *Journal*, 1818–1852

Louis-Philippe at Newhaven. The news of the arrival of the Royal party soon spread among the inhabitants and presently they were visited by Mr Catt of Bishopston tide mills, a Sussex farmer who had

met Louis-Philippe two years earlier when he had gone to the Chateau d'Eu to advise his Majesty on milling in France. 'Ah, Mr Catt,' exclaimed the exile, 'we have had a fearful time of it. We have been eight days in flight and have been within two hours of being murdered. But, thank God, here we are at last on your hospitable shores. It is not the first time, Mr Catt, that I have experienced the generous hospitality of England. I am always proud to come to England.' The farmer offered the Royal party the hospitality of his house at Bishopston, but Louis-Philippe declined the offer with thanks.
Sussex Pictures of the Past, SCM Vol XI, Jan 1937

Seaford has been for some years a favourite resort for excursions of large organized parties – for instance, the Metropolitan Police, the Sunday League, and other bodies; and it must be allowed, whatever the opinion of Sunday excursions may be, or of the question if daily excursions at all are advisable for the welfare of a watering place, that the behaviour of these parties is always quiet, and without the 'Bill and Harry' element showing itself, as occurs sometimes at the seaside during the visits of ordinary excursionists.
W Banks, *Seaford: Past and Present*, 1892

My first customer ran a Curry restaurant in Seaford some 11 miles up the coast from Eastbourne. I spent an hour fixing a terrible Jones machine that really needed to be run over by a dump truck and used as ballast in a boat. By the time I left I stank like a Bombay brothel and I was yearning for a curry...
... My next call was off to The Sisters of Mercy [Annecy School] in Seaford. One of their sisters had returned from Madagascar and, having a passion for sewing, had promptly broken all three of the sewing machines at her convent and then the one next door for good measure! Over the years I have supplied hand machines for their mission in Madagascar where they train people to operate them. The humble sewing machine can mean the difference between a life of poverty and a comfortable living to a local family.
Alex I Askaroff [sewing machine repairman] *Patches of Heaven*, 2001

Travel

Ferry

In 1326 a ferry over the water at 'Beselenebote' by Sefford in Bishopstone was sold for £20 by Robert Le Spicer and Sarah his wife to the Bishop of Chichester who in 1327/8 obtained Royal Licence to transfer it to the Dean and Chapter of Chichester. The custumal of the Bishop's Manor of Bishopstone (1369-85) states that Richard Beselin atte Botte should ferry the Bishop and his carriages and men in his service and all 'avers' (farm beasts) coming from Bishopstone Manor and was to have seven sheaves of wheat during the ferrying of the Bishop from Trachehole to Mechyngwele. In 1409 the Dean and Chapter complained of the expense of the passage of Sefford (probably costs of maintenance and fines for neglect to keep it up).
Sussex Notes and Queries, SAS Vol XVI 1963-67

Horse and Carriage

10th September, 1792. Turnpike. Notice is hereby given that application is intended to be made in the next session of Parliament for an Act to open, widen, amend and repair the road leading from Brighthelmstone to East Bourne through the several parishes of Brighthelmstone, Rottingdean, Telscombe, Piddinghoe, Newhaven, Denton, Bishopstone, Seaford, Alfriston, West Dean, Friston, East Dean, East Bourne all in the County of Sussex. Henry Brooker.
NB. It was intended at first to make the road from Brighthelmstone to Newhaven only, but it has been suggested to the gentlemen concerned that it will be of still greater public utility to extend the road to East Bourne. The above notice as altered is therefore only provisional in case the gentlemen concerned should approve of its being carried to East Bourne.
SMA (TRA2)

17th June, 1793. Seaford diligence through Newhaven to Lewes will commence running on Monday June 17th 1793 and will continue to run every Monday Wednesday Friday and Saturday morning from Seaford during the season to start precisely at 6 o'clock and to arrive at Lewes at 8 o'clock and return from Lewes the same evening to the above places. Performed by the public's most obedient humble servant G Buckley.

Passengers and parcels carefully booked at Mrs Cooke's Seaford, Mr Wymark's Ship Inn, Newhaven, Tubb and Company's Coach Office Lewes.

SMA (TRA2)

Seaford does not boast of any grand buildings, squares, or terraces, calculated to impress the visitor with an exalted sense of its importance: neither is there a cab-stand, or an array of omnibuses, with open doors and noisy conductors, clamorous to bear off the uninitiated on his exit from the railway station, but awaiting instead, and – I contend it is better, cheaper, and safer – the traveller will find a good substantial carriage of somewhat doubtful style and age, drawn by a steady-going horse; and if his coat is bleached from grey to white by years of exposure to a salt atmosphere, he is staunch to the collar, and down hill as good as a dray horse; and are not such qualifications everything? A civil driver in faded livery is ready to take you to your lodgings, if you have any, or to either the New or Old Tree Inn then if you have not. He is a grateful man, this coach-man; he does not get a fare every day, so he practises civility whenever a chance offers itself, lest he should forget the way, and grow too rusty to touch his hat.

W Banks, *Seaford, Past and Present. Handbook and Visitors Guide*, 1892

Cars

Motorists may have received a warning from the spirit world about the dangers of Seaford seafront. Three weeks ago Mr Gordon Spooner, of Buckle Drive, Bishopstone, and his wife Iris, saw a car drive straight into the Seaford sea wall – and disappear.

'It must have been a ghost and I now feel that it could have appeared to us as a message', said Mr Spooner.

He thought the ghost car could have been a warning about the hazardous state of the coast road by Seaford's Martello tower. Since they saw the phantom crash the Spooners have received a number of calls from people with information about fatal accidents at that spot. Now Mr Spooner believes that at least four motorists, including

a doctor and a coastguard, died at the same place. And he thinks he witnessed a ghostly re-enactment of one of the crashes.
Sussex Express, October 1976

Splash, Bang, Wallop! Edith Gladwin, 74, took the plunge when she hit the accelerator instead of the brake as she tried to park her new Nissan Sunny in Seaford on Tuesday. The car shot through a fence and patio doors before nose-diving into a private swimming pool in Maurice Road.

Householder Gill Carpenter and her sister Janet Creasy dived in to push the car to the shallow end as the driver and her husband were trapped inside. The couple inside the car, from Bromley in Kent, were taken to Eastbourne District General Hospital suffering from shock.
Sussex Express, 19.8.1994

You should have gone to Specsavers... The driver of this Vauxhall might want to get his eyes tested after he ploughed straight into an opticians. The crash in Seaford, East Sussex, caused £20,000 of damage yesterday. The 89-year-old's car careered through the display units, coming to a halt in front of three shocked members of staff. Owner Daeron McGee said: 'He was wearing specs but he wasn't one of my customers. He said he had a dizzy turn and hit the accelerator instead of the brake. He smashed through the window and took out about 300 pairs in all.'
Daily Express, 27.6.2009

Motor cycling

The motor cycle and sidecar was also used to fetch visiting officers from the [Newhaven] Railway station, unless of course if they were senior officers, when the Crossley tender was sent. The rating driver of the motor cycle and sidecar discovered that if a little cubbyhole at the back of the sidecar was left open, the door got wedged between the frame and the body, thus putting the suspension out of action and giving the passenger a most uncomfortable ride. Many were the complaints of unpopular passengers who never discovered the cause of their uncomfortable rides.
Peter Fellows, *A Short History of a local Seaplane Station 1917–1920*

A most peculiar procedure was followed (or, more accurately, generally ignored) for paying conductors' takings into the bank. The Southdown office and bank were on the same side of the main road and less than 100 yards apart. It was considered a security risk for the cashier to walk between the two premises, so he had to be driven; Seaford did not have a van or staff car, so a bus would be used. Had the office been before the bank (in respect to direction of traffic flow), it would have been straightforward – draw up outside office, cashier gets on, drive a few yards in straight line, cashier gets off. As it happened, the office was after the bank, which made the operation more complicated. The driver would walk to the garage to collect a spare vehicle, and drive back to the office in a figure-of-eight, passing the bank on the way. With the cash, cashier and spare 'heavies' on board, he would continue in another figure-of-eight to arrive at the bank with it to his near side. By then, he would have driven about 2 miles and turned left or right at eight road junctions. What often happened was that he would momentarily forget the purpose of the mission and sail straight past the bank. If not too deeply engrossed in conversation, the 'security team' would draw

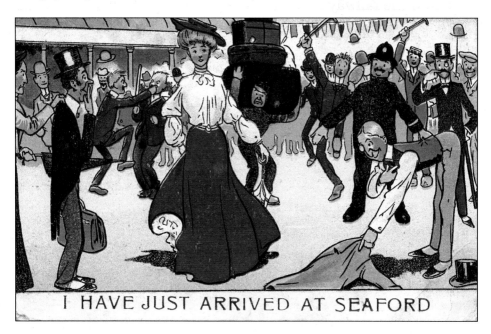

I HAVE JUST ARRIVED AT SEAFORD

his attention to the oversight before he turned off to the garage, and would then walk back to the bank, not too much further than if they had not had a lift to start with!

Bruce Alexander Mcphee, *Works Driver, a view of SOUTHDOWN from the inside*, 2001.

Railways

Extension to Seaford... There seem to have been no obstacles placed in the path of the construction of the line, and opening was announced for 1 June 1864. The line was described as having a bridge over the turnpike at the Buckle Inn with a brick arch 28 ft high; the cutting behind the coast-guard station (Hawth Hill) was 36 ft deep, and the gradients here were 1 in 100. The work had been supervised by the Brighton Company's Engineer FD Banister as Resident Engineer. Free travel was offered on the opening day, and the occasion was marked by ships at Newhaven being fully 'dressed', bunting hung out at the Tide Mills, a procession at Seaford and the usual Dinner.

RW Kidner, *The Newhaven and Seaford Branch*

Somehow the railway has failed to develop it. Yet the spot has great possibilities. It is essentially breezy and only wants a good efficient seawall with a promenade at the top, with bathing establishments, trim gardens and the rest of it, to become as crowded, as expensive, and as disagreeable as all the watering places which really 'pay'. As it is Seaford is a perfect bath of quietude, free from barrel organs, nigger minstrels and dancing boys.

A Visitor of 1876, quoted in Seaford Parish Magazine, October 1926

A branch railway conveys the visitor from Newhaven, and as we whirl along this bright summer afternoon, I can see the sky, the sea, the beach, the snug little village of Blatchington peeping from amidst a group of elms on the extreme left, and a furzy knoll, on which stands a flagstaff, some distance ahead...

W Banks, *Seaford: Past and Present*, 1892

The station [Bishopstone] was designed around an octagonal booking hall with projecting wings with rounded brickwork; typical of 1930s design...

The new station was opened on September 26, 1938 and the same day the old Bishopstone Beach Station was closed. The modern new station was built of brick and concrete but soon had to be altered due to the demands of war. In 1940 the octagonal tower was turned into a well disguised military pillbox with two projecting areas each having recessed gun-slits facing both towards the sea and inland. This part of the new design is similar to that of a 'type 27 pillbox' which was a brick built octagonal fortified structure usually used to defend airfields. A small military camp was built south of the station (on the site now occupied by a caravan site) and the station was busy with the comings and goings of soldiers based there...

Bishopstone station, a classic art-deco design, is now a Grade II listed building.

Kevin Gordon, *From A Seaford Album*, Sussex Express 25.5.2006

Air

The old tide mills site was a seaplane base in the First World War and was used for close quarter battle training in the Second World War when the whole of the sea front was a restricted area in anticipation of another invasion.

John Odam, *Bygone Seaford*

Observer Martin Press survived four forced landings, all with different pilots. Normally the patrols cruised at a thousand feet looking for submarines and Press reckoned that if the engine stopped at that height, he could send out an SOS and his call sign three times before alighting on the sea. He would then scribble a message on special paper, roll it in a tiny aluminium cylinder, clip it on a pigeon's leg and release the bird. The bird, having been in a small space and sleepy after perhaps 3 or 4 hours, took a poor view of flying. Thrown up into the air, it would circle and then land on the wing tip. It had to be frightened off by throwing Lewis Gun rounds at it, being careful not to hit the bird that might save them! Providing a hungry sportsman did not shoot it down, the pigeon would get to the squadron in due course.

Peter Fellows, *A Short History of a local Seaplane Station 1917–1920*

The schools could together wield a considerable influential force in the town's affairs... An excellent example of such power and influence was revealed in 1933 when there was a proposal to build an aerodrome at Seaford on the Sutton Fields site... The strip would not be used for large airliners, but rather for light machines, carrying no more than six persons, it was also emphasised that planes would not fly over the schools. However, there was a great deal of opposition voiced by the Schools' Association... Opposition came from other head-masters and mistresses, who were anxious not to see an aerodrome in Seaford. Miss Cameron of the Downs School, said she had one hundred and thirty pupils, some of whom were delicate and absolute quiet was essential... Mr Brewer, headmaster of Chesterton, said that one of his parents had said; 'If an aerodrome came to Seaford my two boys would have to leave your school'.

...The Schools' Association was successful in their appeal, and the proposal for an aerodrome was rejected.

Katharine H Ridley, *Schools in Seaford, East Sussex* (SMA)

Space Travel

Piers [Sellers] was born in Crowborough in 1955 and at the age of four attended Tyttenhanger Lodge Pre-Preparatory School on the Eastbourne Road in Seaford. While at the school, he was asked what he wanted to do when he grew up. He firmly replied that he wanted to be a spaceman – and how right he was... He joined NASA in 1996 and six years later undertook his first space mission on board the space station when he took part in his first space walk. On his current mission he has to undertake three spacewalks in order to construct and test various items of scientific equipment. During Saturday's walk he was attached to the end of a long robotic arm (which he described as a fishing-rod) and was able to look back at the space station and marvel as the earth spun slowly underneath him.

Kevin Gordon, *From A Seaford Album*, 14.7.2006

Societies and Entertainments

I recall one [Debating Society] which flourished for a short spell at any rate, in Sussex nearly forty years ago and had a membership approaching two hundred and fifty ... Prominent men in the district gave their active support and we soon attracted representatives of all shades of opinion... Lord Rosebery, perhaps the greatest orator of his day, wrote: 'If your Seaford Model Parliament teaches you only to debate and deliver speeches it will be a curse to you. If it teaches you to think for yourselves it will be a blessing. The choice will be with your members.'

The interest of the ladies was aroused by a letter from Miss Sylvia Pankhurst, the Suffragette Campaigner, hoping that the Seaford Parliament would transact its affairs in a more businesslike way than that at Westminster, and would lose no time in giving women the Parliamentary vote!

Morley Stuart, *Memories of a Seaford Model Parliament*

Bonfire past and present

5th November 1867. The anniversary of the Gunpowder Plot was celebrated in this town in a manner which rather astonished the natives... First in the procession came the Captain in full regimentals, sabre in hand; then his lieutenants and staff carrying torches and coloured lights. Behind these came the Seaford fife and drum band, backed up by a large banner, on which was inscribed in large letters, 'Seaford Bonfire Boys', a blazing hogshead, drawn by six men, and guarded by six torch bearers came next, and behind this more torch barrels, and another banner 'God Save the Queen'. The rear of the procession was brought up by a body of fishermen. At the termination of the second procession the boat was set on fire and two tar barrels pitched into it. The result was a glorious fire, and around this an immense crowd congregated and squibs and crackers were flying in all directions. At 12 o'clock the last grand procession ended; the captain previous to retiring made a short speech, in which he thanked the bonfire boys for the orderly manner in which they had conducted the processions, and congratulated them in the success of the whole affair (immense cheering, and from the band, 'For he's a jolly good fellow'). Thus ended the evening of the 5th November,

and we are happy to say that all passed off to the entire satisfaction of all parties, and great praise is due to those who had the management of the processions for the order which pervaded the whole evening. We believe one timid individual sent for six policemen but his fears were groundless. He was like 'the wicked which flee when no man pursueth them'.
Sussex Express, 9.11.1867, SMA (RN)

5th November 1883. Thanks to the energetic action taken by Captain Crook, there was a grand display here on Monday evening, the great feature of the evening being the construction of a high fortress on the Beamelands, in front of which were two lines of fortifications, and it was arranged that a miniature battle should be fought by the boys, who were divided into attacking and defending parties. The defenders were armed; in addition to rockets, shells, etc, with a number of rifles and cannons, and for a time the contest raged merrily; but eventually the defenders had to retire from one line of defence to another, until they were overpowered and their stronghold captured. Before the attacking party could obtain possession, however, the tower was set on fire, and burned furiously for a time. A quantity of combustibles had been deposited in the fortress, and as these exploded the effect was remarkably good. The surrounding district was brilliantly illuminated, while the crack of rifles, the thunder of the cannon, and the dispersion of the crowd by 'rousers', made up a scene which is more easily imagined than described. Such an excellent display has rarely been witnessed at Seaford...
Sussex Express, 10.11.1883, SMA (RN)

Thousands turned out to enjoy Seaford Bonfire Society's bash on Saturday, following the organisation's revival. The much-awaited event saw people from Seaford and beyond turn out to watch the torch-lit procession. Former stuntman and local resident Eddie Kidd was on hand to fire a signal to start the parade from the White Lion pub... Among the tableaux created by the society were the head of King Alfred, a skull and crossbones and a large Seaford Shag, the bird from which the society takes its name... A huge bonfire was built at the Martello Fields and there was an amazing firework display by local company Frontier Fireworks watched by a huge crowd. Society chairman Steve Russell complimented all who took

part, adding: 'The procession was unbelievable and it was fantastic to see not only the variety of costumes but also the happy looks of the crowds as we passed.'
Seaford Gazette, 26.10.2011

Cinemas

The Empire Cinema, situated in the centre of the Town, is in every way up-to-date. The seating is comfortable and the programme consistently maintains a high standard, with the latest and best Talking Pictures. 'Phone 355.
Sunny Seaford, Official Publicity Bureau, 1936

At the height of a fierce blaze which gutted the Empire Cinema, Seaford, early on Wednesday morning, a 50-ft water tower being used by the Seaford Fire Brigade, crashed to the ground, and Fireman Fred Mace, who was strapped to the top if it, received fatal injuries.

All that remains of the cinema, which was insured for £14,000, are four blackened brick walls and the booking office.
Sussex Express and County Herald, 3 March 1939

A plaque was unveiled at the weekend in memory of a Seaford fireman after his family called for a fitting tribute to be created in his honour. The family of Frederick Mace joined Seaford MP Norman Baker and Seaford mayor Councillor Tracy Willis on Saturday for the ceremony... Town crier Peter White travelled to the unveiling on a preserved 1939 fire engine which originated from Newhaven...
Seaford Gazette, 3.3.2010

The Ritz was very well equipped for toilets considering its reasonably modest size. There was the set for the circle, a set in the lower foyer, and a further set in the splay walls on either side of the proscenium. No expense was spared, even here. The men's toilets were fully tiled in an attractive shade of green, and the ladies were pink. Some tiles had a design representing wave formations, or some other motif of the sea on them, and these were worked into the overall design. The sea feature was a recurring theme in the interior decorations of the Ritz.

...In the summer of 1977, Myles Byrne was persuaded by one Bill Byrne to go into partnership and present a summer ice show at the Ritz called The Jubilee Ice Show of 1977. It opened on Monday July 25th and folded after just two weeks. It was dreadful. The ice pad was a tiny 27ft by 24ft, the total cast, both chorus and principals, numbered just twelve and the lighting was provided by nothing more than the old number one batten, hastily slung in front of the proscenium, over the front stalls where the ice pad had been constructed. The whole production was hopelessly under-financed. On Monday August 8th films re-commenced. It had been predicted that the ice show would run for six weeks, but only half a dozen or so members of the public supported the daily 2.30 and 8.00 pm performances and the summer spectacular could not continue.
[The Ritz Cinema finally closed down in 1980. Morrison's supermarket now occupies the site]
Picture House, No 9, Winter 1986

Theatre

After the end of the war in 1945, Valerie Sheppard and friends first established the Seaford Dramatic Society. In the beginning they rehearsed in various halls and in each other's houses, built the scenery in garages and hired the Clinton Hall (now flats) to carry out dress rehearsals and performances. This was a lot of hard work for the members as most of them had daytime jobs. They continued like this until 1949, when the Christian Science halls in Steyne Road came up for sale... To pay the £1000 asked for by the halls a plan of £1 shares was proposed to the members, who rallied to the call and so the Little Theatre was born.
Stella Dench, *The History of Seaford Little Theatre*, May 2008 SMA (RN3)

The Seaford Musical Theatre Juniors shone in their first ever production – 'Jessie's Dream' – performed at the Barn Theatre, Seaford at the end of October... With just 12 weeks to write, choreograph and stage the show with a cast of mainly first-time performers aged between 8-16, many lesser directors would have trembled but stage veteran Paula Woolven loved the challenge... 'It really was THEIR show', Paula said, 'from the idea to the characters to the costumes and dancing – I just helped by putting the script together.' It was colourful, energetic and extremely entertaining! The audience were up on their feet at every performance. I loved the fact that the children wanted to show how different society and music has become over the last forty years. With songs from Abba squaring off against Lady Gaga and Donny Osmond vs Bruno Mars, the music delighted every member of the audience of all generations... A replica of one of the first massive mobile phones, Lady Gaga's out-rageous lobster hats and a poster of the Bay City Rollers are now put away in the SMT Juniors props box and they are all looking forward to starting rehearsals for their next show 'Carry On up the Beanstalk', a musical pantomime which will be staged in March 2012.

Seaford Scene, December 2011

Sports, Games, Hobbies and Celebrations

Here is fishing, bathing, rowing, sailing, lounging, running, pic-nicing, and a cook who builds a basis of strength to make us equal to all these superhuman efforts.

Letters of George Meredith, 1857

PUBLIC RECREATION GROUNDS facing the Esplanade, provided with Hard and Grass Courts and Bowling Green, Miniature Golf Course for the use of visitors, a Play-ground for children, including a Pond for paddle-boats and model yachts. A man is in constant attendance.

Sunny Seaford, Sussex, Official Publicity Bureau, 1936

Coronation of King George VI and Queen Elizabeth, 12th May 1937

10.15 am United Service of Prayer and Thanksgiving on the "Salts" Recreation Ground. All Denominations (if wet, in the Ritz Cinema). 11.00 am. Fancy Dress and Decorated Vehicles parade on Esplanade, commencing at Stafford Road and proceeding to Marine Parade. Prizes for Decorated Horse Carts, Commercial and Private Cars, Cycles, Ladies', Gentleman's and Children's Fancy Dresses. 12.15 pm Luncheon at the Queen's Hall for Old Folks of 68 years and over.

1.15 pm Sports for Children and Adults on the "Salts" Recreation Ground. Valuable Prizes. No Entrance Fee.

4.30 pm Tea at the Queen's Hall for all Children over 4 and under 15 years of age. A Souvenir Coronation Mug will be presented to each child.

9.00 pm Torchlight Procession. Commencing from Queen's Hall and proceeding to top of Seaford Head to light the Bonfire. Torches will be provided.

10.00 pm Dance at the Queen's Hall until 3.30 am. Admission 1/- to cover cost of Refreshments.

Souvenir Programme, Urban District of Seaford, ESRO AMS 6136/51

Bowls

The clergy preached against Sunday Sport and all the associated denominational societies discussed the issue and voted against it, not entirely without some opposition, although that was disguised in anonymity. A 'Publican and Sinner' wrote to the local paper to say that Luther and Calvin had played bowls on Sunday and that the 'opponents on Sunday play object to it in much the same way as Macaulay says that the Puritans objected to bull-baiting... because it gave pleasure to the spectators'.

An Embryonic Brighton? Victorian and Edwardian Seaford, ed John Lowerson

The Crouch Bowling Club has flourished and today its 74 members can look back on many successes. Unhappily no club records prior to 1942 remain in existence, because the then Secretary, George Borrisow, and the Vice-Captain, Bill Tomley, were both killed by enemy action. The club records and some trophies were destroyed in the same air raid.

Oliver Watson, *The Crouch Bowling Club, Seaford*, SMA (RN16) c 1960

The new club [The Seaford Bowls Club] was officially opened on 30th April 1949 and the splendid new green attracted new membership...

There were problems with vandalism during the 1978 season when holes were dug into the green on several occasions. Night time vigils were responsible for catching the culprits – two foxes.

Kevin Gordon, *From A Seaford Album*, Sussex Express 03.10.08

Golf

The golf links had been laid out in 1887 and stretched from Chyngton Road across Seaford Head, with tees and holes dangerously near the cliff edge in places. Another hazard on the Head was sheep. If they were cropping the grass on the approach to the eighth a player must not just shout 'Fore' and play through them. He or she, for there was a nine hole course for the ladies, was required to find the shepherd, Reuben Russell, and request him to remove his charges. This he would do, no doubt for a consideration, just as his wife would cook whatever the golfers had brought in the way of lamb chops and beef steaks for their lunches. She did so on her own stove for her cottage was used as the golf club house, until members moved first into corrugated iron huts and then to more spacious quarters.

John Odam, *The Seaford Story 1000–2000 AD*

The decision to play golf on Sunday was not universally approved – a haughty letter from a Seaford churchgoer published in the local paper said 'a man who played golf on a Sunday would not be particular whether he paid his debts or not'. It was even suggested that should Sunday play be allowed, the character of Seaford would be forever affected and families would cease to use the town as a seaside resort.

Kevin Gordon, *From a Seaford Album*, Sussex Express 14.1.2010

Marbles

On Good Friday it was the custom at Seaford and elsewhere to play marbles in and around the churchyard. This is said by some to be the sole remaining part of the Pre-Reformation Passion Play and to represent the Roman soldiers gambling at the foot of the Cross. My own opinion is that it is far more likely to be a survival of the funeral games played in most pagan countries in the distant past around and upon the graves of notable persons on the anniversary of their deaths.

Sussex Notes and Queries, SAS Vol X, 1944–1945

I remember one occasion when my father, hearing that there was to be a match at Seaford between Public and Private School men, drove over to witness it.

On appearing on the ground he was at once seized upon by the Public School team and entreated to play as one of their number had at the last moment suddenly failed them. He pleaded that he had given over playing for many years. Then he pointed out a piece of water, which he said did not allow of a large enough field. Both sides laughed at the idea of the possibility of sending a ball as far as the water. In the end my father was persuaded to play. When batting, on the first opportunity he had, he sent his ball into the middle of the sheet of water, where it could be seen floating about, and so could not be called a lost ball. On that ball my father obtained twenty-four runs before anybody waded into the water after it.

Rev Edward Boys Ellman, *Recollections of a Sussex Parson* 1925

We were pleased to welcome Jack Hobbs here on June 27th. He coached the first eleven all the afternoon, and later had a knock himself. Our thanks are due to him for his present to the school of an autograph group of the MCC Australian Team.

King's Mead Terminal Letters, Summer Term 1929, SMA (Schools)

Sussex had struggled to find a wicketkeeper who could contribute consistent runs since Moores retired in 1998. Shaun Humphries and Nick Wilton were both excellent glove men, but neither made a first-class hundred. [Matt] Prior arrived on the staff in 2001 through conventional routes – he had first worked with Moores as a 12-year-old when he joined Sussex's junior set-up – but the same could not be said of [Tim] Ambrose. In fact, had it not been for the persistence of an aunt in Seaford, he might have been lost to Sussex, and English, cricket forever.

Brian Talbot and Paul Weaver, *Flight of the Martlets, The Golden Age of Sussex Cricket*

Football

The future of STFC's League fortunes – or at least its ability to comply with the FA's rules for what a ground has to have before the team can win promotion, no matter how well they play – was hotly debated twice in the 2000's. A somewhat crass strategy of being rude to everyone who disagreed ensured that local residents and councillors united to reject permission to put up floodlights; a change of management and tactics eventually won over sufficient support at the second attempt. Current players and supporters might care to note that the campaign also spawned the Crouch Potatoes' song 'Seaford Town' which still sounds fresh.

Seaford Town Football Club, http://www.stfc.org.uk/about1.htm

Rugby

Seaford Rugby Football Club was originally founded in 1938 with Sir George Coldstream as president. The first game played by the newly formed club was against Lewes Priory, losing 40-nil! Fortunes improved and the club finished the season with a record of 13 wins, nine losses and one draw. During this season, the club colours were blue and white the home pitch being at King's Mead School,

The onset of the Second World war led to the closure of the club, but it was reformed in 1951. At that point, the colours were changed to red and white, games were played at Newlands School with changing facilities provided by the Seven Sisters pub – the showers supplied via a hosepipe from the garden shed.

SMA [Sporting Exhibition 2012]

Skating

The School had a most enjoyable time during the great frost. They spent every available spare minute on the ice. About forty of them were able to skate at the end of the ten days. Several boys skated along the Cuckmere from Exceat Bridge to the sea. The Ouse above Newhaven and the pond at Bishopstone both provided good ice, and the last day all boys with skates went to Firle Park, taking their lunch with them.

King's Mead Terminal Letters, Easter Term 1929, SMA (Schools)

Races

8 March 1848... I forgot to put down yesterday that I saw a throng of men and boys collected on the Common between Seaford and Corsica Lodge, and on inquiry found that a wheelbarrow race for a Cock was going on: the Seaford Shrovetide pastime from time immemorial.
Rev Robert Nathaniel Dennis, *Diaries*

Bathing

A number of well-appointed bathing machines are placed on the beach. For those who are swimmers, the water being cleaner than where there is a sand shore, the bathing is most agreeable at all times of tide, while at low tide the most timid may go out a long distance on sand with perfect safety.

Boats and fishing gear may be hired, whiting, conger, mackerel, and other species of fish being generally plentiful in their several seasons. The most splendid prawns are to be caught among the rocks under the cliffs, and Seaford shrimps are fine.
W Banks, *Seaford: Past and Present. Handbook and Visitors' Guide*, 1892

6. A person shall not at any time use for the purpose of bathing therefrom without a bathing machine any part of the sea-shore except the public bathing places appointed for the purpose in pursuance of the Byelaw in that behalf.
7. Every person shall at all times while bathing wear suitable drawers or other sufficient dress or covering to prevent indecent exposure of the person.
Public Bathing, Urban District Council of Seaford Byelaws 1911, SMA

Ballooning

BALLOON-MAKING AT SEAFORD [Richmond Road]
In our View of Mr [Henry] Coxwell's manufactory, a new balloon lying in the centre of the floor is just undergoing the sewing of the last seam by the sempstresses. A workman is in the act of turning the wheel of a wind-machine, the effect of which is to separate the gores and to throw the balloon into an elongated form preparatory

for examination. The appendages to his aeronautic machines are in close proximity, in the shape of netting, grapnels, cars, and other appurtenances. Laid up in a packed condition are six of the celebrated aeronaut's balloons, which include the Research and another in which ascents were made on behalf of the British Association with Mr Glaisher, when an elevation of seven miles was obtained. Green's famous old balloon, The Nassau, is also here in dock, and several others with which Mr Coxwell has frequently ascended.

The Penny Illustrated Paper, SMA (P)

Balloon Ascent: Mr Coxwell, the aeronaut, and Mr F J Ashton, made an ascent today from Lewes with the balloon [Jem?], the property of Mr Ashton. Two pilot balloons went straight away in the direction of Tunbridge Wells, and a start was made at 5.20 in a most favourable state of the atmosphere; and when the balloon rose, amid the cheers of the spectators, it took the direction intended. Shortly after it met with a northerly current and was carried towards sea, when it was deemed advisable to descend. The descent was made satisfactorily, shortly before 7, 2 miles from Seaford.

The Times, 30.5.1876

Glaisher wrote: 'On emerging from the cloud at 1hr 17m we came into a flood of light, with a beautiful blue sky without a cloud above us and a magnificent sea of cloud below.' Two hours later he passed out and Coxwell managed to free the ropes required to make their descent by tugging at them with his teeth as his hands had become frozen... In June 1880 Coxwell became the first man to make 1,000 balloon ascents. He made his last flight five years later. He died in 1900 aged 81 and his widow erected a memorial to him in St Peter's Church, Blatchington. The memorial calls him a 'famous aeronaut' and, maybe because of his success at altitude, the memorial is placed quite high up within the church.

Kevin Gordon, *From a Seaford Album,* Sussex Express 14.7.2006

Birdwatching

I have said that the only sea-bird that now breeds on the cliffs along the southern edge of the South Downs is the herring-gull. Their most interesting colony is at Seaford Head where I have observed them during the last three summers... In the first week of June I had the good fortune to see the gulls at this spot in a new and beautiful aspect. At the top of the cliff, where it is about four hundred feet high, a quantity of earth has fallen or crumbled away leaving a gap about thirty to forty feet deep, and into this I crept and placed myself as near the edge as I could safely get. Lying there perfectly still, the birds, which had been flying up and down before me uttering their loud anxious cries, began to settle on all the near projecting pieces of chalk where they could watch me. By-and-by I had twenty-four of them all perched close to me, in pairs or small groups of three or four, some of them standing on the chalk where it was partly overgrown with patches of sea-pink, or thrift. The intense whiteness of the sunlit chalk and rosy red of the numerous flat little flowers gave a novel and very beautiful appearance to the birds. For they were very near, and quite motionless, though clamouring with open beaks and swollen throats, and all their colours were clearly visible – the white and tender pale grey of the plumage, the shining yellow eye and yellow beak, with its orange-red patch on the lower mandible, and the flesh-coloured legs.
WH Hudson, *Nature in Downland*, 1923

THE SEA

Splash Point and Seaford Bay

Chaotic, spume sprayed,
Seaweed-slippy,
Sea-sculpted stones
Bar the way
To invaders

And a schizophrenic sea,
Gentle opalescence
Or mad-dog foamed,
Confirms the anarchy
Of the elements

Peter Martin, extract from *Ghost Music*

Here, at a place called Splash Point, four or five pairs of kittiwakes started to nest in 1976, and since then their numbers have increased, fluctuating between 50 to 300 pairs. They nest in colonies on cliff ledges and once the site becomes overcrowded many pairs leave to form new colonies nearby... Like the fulmar petrel, the kittiwake is a truly oceanic species, spending much of its time amongst the waves of the deep Atlantic, coming to our coasts in February and March to breed. What an attractive bird to watch at this time, as they pair up, standing close together, breasts inwards and touching the cliff face and each other... Their courtship exchanges are delightful; graceful bowing of heads to each other, and gentle fondling movements with their bills, all accompanied by excited mewing calls.

Patrick Coulcher, *Unto the Hills*

The bay, with its bold sweep, between the heights of Newhaven on the west and those of Seaford Cliff on the east, presents a spectacle of great beauty, especially during the prevalence of an easterly wind, when it is often literally studded with vessels of various sizes and nations, unable to make their way round the dangerous promontory of Beachy Head, about six miles eastward. As many as two hundred sail have been known to be thus detained for days together.

MA Lower, *Notes on Seaford*, 1868

Seaward it is dead low water; the smooth ocean lies breathing in the sunlight like some sleeping monster; only the tiniest of waves curl over the shingle, the fishing boats are everyone hauled high and dry upon the shore, whilst in the offing a boat may be seen idling along, or a column of dark smoke pointing out the course of some steamer, bound either up or down channel.

W Banks, *Seaford: Past and Present* 1892

The Beach

Today it has been 'blust'rous', as they say here. The water within a foot of our little one room and surf raging up wrathful-white all along the shingle and breaking in feathery masses on the sulphur gray curtain of cloud... Blatchington beach is battered to bits.

The Letters of George Meredith, 15.10.1856

16th May 1860

I have received from the Solicitor to this Department his Report with reference to the claim of the Corporation of Seaford to the foreshore in front of their Borough...The evidence against the Corporation apart from the prima facie right of the Crown, appears to consist in the facts that the grant of 34th Elizabeth, on which the Corporation must necessarily rely, is not conceived in terms which would ordinarily have been employed at that time, or which would now be employed, to pass foreshore between high and low water marks, that for the last thirty six years everyone who pleased has taken sand and shingle from the shore in question – and that, where the Corporation have perambulated the boundaries of the borough the foreshore has never been included within it.

Under these circumstances I do not feel warranted in recommending that the claim of the Corporation should be admitted, but as I am persuaded they only wish to do what is right in the matter, and as it is very desirable, with a view to enable either the Crown, or the Corporation speedily and effectively to prevent the evil arising from the removal of boulders, shingle, and sand from the foreshore in front of the Borough of Seaford, that a determination of the question, as to the right to such foreshore, should be arrived at with as little delay as possible...

Letter from Charles Gore, ESRO SEA/517

Perhaps inevitably, the prospect of promenading visitors attracted some buskers and Punch and Judy men and, eventually, a touring Pierrot troupe. In keeping with tradition, this latter group gave impromptu performances on the beach to the accompaniment of a portable piano, taking a collection afterwards. It may have amused the holidaymakers, but it incensed the manager of the Seaford Bay Estate. In mid-September, 1894, he took abrupt action against the Lyric Trio, using the cover of the law of trespass. Since the troupe were on the Company's beach, he ejected them with a force of 20 strong-arm men, who carried the portable piano away, to dump it

several streets away off the Company's land. His justification was that several residents and visitors had complained about the doubtful nature of some of the performers' songs.

An Embryonic Brighton? Victorian and Edwardian Seaford, ed. John Lowerson

Ship Building and Fishing

By the close of the 13th Century Seaford had a larger number of wool merchants than Chichester, Lewes, Shoreham, and Winchelsea, the number of local ships inferring a considerable ship-building industry and it is under these prosperous conditions in 1298 that the towns recorded contributions to Cinque ports armaments begin. This date coincides with the year in which the Town first sent its Members to Parliament. Seaford was the only Limb of the entire confederation which ever enjoyed this privilege, granted, it is said, by Edward I in return for the inhabitants placing five ships at his disposal for some special naval venture.

Seaford: A Member of the Cinque Ports Liberty of Hastings, Seaford Museum

Seaford grew rapidly as a thriving, maritime commercial centre, and soon it overshadowed its senior Saxon neighbours of Sutton, East Blatchington and Chyngton. By the 13th Century Seaford's trade, as a Sussex port, seems to have been exceeded only by that of Chichester and Winchelsea. Southdown wool was the principal export. Flanders and Holland were the main customers. By the end of that century, Shoreham and Chichester led Seaford, but some interesting points now begin to emerge. Other Sussex and Kent ports used both English and alien vessels to carry on this trade, but Seaford used English vessels only. These were probably all Seaford built and Seaford manned ships, and this pre-supposes quite an extensive ship building industry, presumably carried on where houses and flats today stand adjacent to the former river bed.

... Perhaps the great storm of 1579 finally sealed the Seaford exit for ever, and by 1580 Seaford was being described as 'a duckpool'. Records of the former Seaford Corporation quote the last will and testament of Robert Callards, who died in 1592. He was described as 'a shipwright', probably the last of that line in Seaford. The stock and tools of his trade, by then virtually valueless, he left to his sons.

Edna and Mac McCarthy, *Sussex River, Seaford to Newhaven*

By the Comm[ission?] for Executing the Office of Lord High Admiral of Great Britain and Ireland:

These are to give Notice that no Fishermen or others employed in the fishery at Seaford, during this Season are to be impressed into his Majesty's Service, but permitted to follow their said Employment without any Lett, hindrance or molestation whereunto all Commanders, Officers, Press Masters and others whom it doth or may concern are to have due regard. Given under our hand and the seal of the office of Admiralty the 20th May 1740.

By Command of their Lordships   [3 signatures]
Admiralty
ESRO SEA/490

Seaford June 17th 1788
The humble Petition of Stephen Green of the Place aforesaid an Industrious Fisherman with a very large Family sheweth that in an hard gale of wind he had the misfortune to lose all his mackerel nets to the Amount of twenty Pounds and upwards – which has lost him the present Mackerel season and reduced him and his numerous Family to the greatest distress – the Contributions of his Friends will therefore be thankfully received, and your Petitioner as in Duty bound will ever pray –
Stephen Green – His Mark X
List of 21 subscribers pledging from 5 shillings up to a guinea each
ESRO SEA/701

Facilities for a fishery on an extensive scale exist here, and enterprise and capital would be well rewarded were they properly employed. It may be remarked that a large proportion of the fish caught by the Brighton, Hastings and Eastbourne fishermen are taken in this bay... should a branch railway be formed (which might easily and inexpensively be done) to connect it with Newhaven and the South Coast Line, few watering places would be more eagerly sought after by visitors; or better repay the exertions of enterprising capitalists.
MA Lower, *Memorials of Seaford,* 1855

Cinque Ports and Sea Battles

About the year 1293, in the reign of King Edward I, a hundred vessels of the Cinque ports fought at sea with a great fleet of French ships, and although were overwhelmed in numbers, they slew, sunk, and took so many of them that France was for a long season after destitute of both seamen and shipping.
WR Wynter, *Old Seaford*

For the campaign of Crecy and the siege of Calais [1346] a large armament was collected – from 1,000 to 1,600 sail, say the chroniclers. According to the Roll of Calais, which purports to be a copy of a Wardrobe Account of Edward III, the fleet gathered for the siege including 21 ships and 596 men from Winchelsea, 9 ships and 156 men from Rye, 5 ships and 96 men from Hastings, 20 ships and 329 men from Shoreham, and 5 ships and 80 men from Seaford.
Maritime History, The Victoria History of Sussex, 1905

The seals of the Ports are of particular interest, since most of them carry a representation of a Cinque ports ship. Most of the towns in the Confederation either possess, or once possessed, several of different periods, the earliest ones being somewhat crude and simple, but many of the later ones are crisp and full of detail... As might be expected later seals are fine, with much fuller detail as a general rule. Tenterden's mid-15th century common seal shows a single-masted ship with a square sail carrying the Cinque ports motif of the half lions and half ships, but perhaps the most detailed is the 1544 common seal of Seaford. This shows in some detail, a Tudor three-masted ship with a crow's nest of each tapered mast, rope ladders, and details of the rigging.
Ivan Green, *The Book of the Cinque Ports*

Lewes, Sussex Feb 23rd – On Saturday the *Sky*, a French Privateer, fell in with the *Furnace Bomb*, a 20 gun-ship off Seaford about Eleven o'Clock in the morning and was taken about Five in the afternoon after a short engagement. The said privateer had on board 62 men, besides officers, which are present confined in Seaford Church [St Leonard's] and the officers are kept on board.

She has used this coast for some time as a smuggling Cutter and so made prey of everything she could lay hands on. The captain is Swiss.

Derby Mercury, 27th February 1746

[A privateer is a government sponsored pirate ship]

A recently discovered document, obtained from the records of certain litigation resulting from a dispute respecting the division of prize-money tells how on 21st May 1747, the captain of the *St Paul*, merchant-ship, bound from London to Virginia with £23,000 worth of valuables, descried a French privateer making for his ship. In order to escape the Frenchman, the *St Paul* was run aground in Cuckmere Bay, where the water was too shallow to allow the enemy to come alongside. Despite this, the French put off in boats, and succeeded in capturing the *St Paul*. However, the incident had been witnessed by certain persons on shore, who at once opened fire upon the captured merchant-ship, with the object of preventing the French from carrying off the treasure. Fresh arms and ammunition being forthcoming from Seaford, boats were obtained, twenty-three of the captors were taken, and the privateer set sail, leaving the *St Paul* and the prisoners in the hands of the Sussex men.

Arthur Beckett, *The Spirit of the Downs*, 1949

Seaford, 29th December 1755

... People are now pretty much unconcerned about the French, as the sea has been very rough for some time past, but when that [eases?] 'tis probable their old Pannicks will return.

Letter from John Hubbersty to his brother John, ESRO AMS 6126/13

Capture of a French Privateer. (December 19th 1796). Last Wednesday between 8 and 9 o'clock in the evening Captain Simmons of His Majesty's armed cutter the *Lion* belonging to Hastings, captured off Seaford after a chase of four hours and a half a French cutter privateer called the *Hazard*, commanded by Captain La Mair. The *Lion* brought her prize into Seaford and there landed her prisoners. The captain underwent an examination before the Bailiff, from which it appears that he had [spent] two days before fitting out at Fécamp and sailed from Dieppe but without having taken anything. Had he escaped the *Lion* his intention was to have come to anchor in Seaford bay, for the purpose of cutting out a Dover sloop which he observed lying there. The *Hazard* mounted two carriage guns and two swivel guns, and had on board seventeen hands including officers and a number of small arms. The prisoners are lodged in the black hole at Seaford until an order arrives for their removal to Deal or to some other place of great security.

SMA (LO)

It was on Innocents' Day, Dec 28, in the year 1807, that the Downsmen who lived along the coast between Beachy Head and Newhaven saw a stirring sight, the fight of a small English coal-carrying vessel, a 'collier' and a large French privateer bristling with guns and other armaments...

It only needed one broadside from the privateer to put the hulking collier out of action and send it to the bottom. But that broadside never came. Either the Frenchman hoped to secure a second prize as undamaged as the first, or, what was more likely, had been so confident of an unresisting capture that her guns were still limbered and before she had time to loosen and man them, the collier had a second chance and used it. She was then close to the Frenchman and the guns this time played with deadly affect. For at this volley the shot was aimed below the privateer's water-line, tearing great holes, into which the water poured, and at the same time the sturdy collier bumped into her, cutting a deep vertical wound in her hull.

That was the end of the smart French clipper. In a few minutes she had sunk in the bay, carrying with her nearly 100 men, of which – so swiftly did she submerge – the gallant little collier was only able with its dinghy to pick up five of the crew. The fight was witnessed by a huge crowd which had now gathered round the bay and on the hills from Newhaven to Seaford.

The Rev AA Evans, *A Christmas Fight Off Seaford Head*, SCM Vol 1, 1927

Wrecks

It was the firing of the cannons to warn the fleet of pending danger that woke the inhabitants of Seaford that morning [7th December 1809], who then flocked to the long stretch of shingle, unable to do much in the thick fog. As streaks of daylight broke through the true horror became apparent. Five ships lay near the *Harlequin* at the east end of the bay and half a mile or so further east was the seventh, the *Weymouth*. The *Sussex Weekly Advertiser* reported, 'They beheld the spectacle that was truly dreadful, the seven ships being high together and complete wrecks, with the remaining crews clinging to differing parts of them, imploring for assistance which is natural in such cases.'

Wendy Hughes, *Shipwrecks of Sussex*

On St Valentine's Day in 1882 the freighter *SS Gannett* bound for London from Calcutta laden with a cargo of coffee, cotton, grain, tea and spices from the East was wrecked in a storm in Seaford Bay. Thankfully, the crew were brought safely ashore by breeches-buoy. In the process one of the officers who was entrusted with the ship's manifest etc took a soaking from the heavy seas. The papers which he was carrying got saturated. On dry land fortunately a young chambermaid at the [Seaford Bay] Hotel came to his rescue by helping him dry them out. They fell in love, married and he took her out to India with him on his next voyage.

Joan EV Redman, *A Pint Pot of Old Seaford*

Diary: Wednesday Feb 22nd 1882
Went down on the beach to see the ship *Gannet* that is ashore nearly opposite the Martello Tower, a large steam (iron) ship, the beach was like a fair with horses and men, the cargo of tea, cotton, linseed, hides [?] etc was carried in farm waggons up to the station, several policemen were in attendance. Went along the sea wall which is only just wide enough to walk on in places, it not being all filled in with chalk. Scrambled up the face of this cliffe into the place where the men are excavating the chalk from the wall. Went down to the ship again in the afternoon...

Thursday February 23rd
Went twice to the ship, saw the Captain who is a very mean looking little man...

Wednesday Dec 5th 1883
...walked by the river to Seaford direct along by the beach and saw where the sea has washed away the whole front of the battery.
Diary of Ruth Caroline Morris née Verral, ESRO AMS 6572/6/1

On this day, February 8, 90 years ago, a south-westerly gale was blowing when the steel-hulled Danish sailing barque *Peruvian* ran aground opposite the Esplanade hotel. She was on her way to Hamburg after crossing the Atlantic from Ecuador, with a cargo of logwood and 'vegetable ivory' – nuts from a South American palm – destined for the button-factories of Europe.

...At last, the lifeboat, powered only by oarsmen, manoeuvred between the ship and the beach and took off nine men and the captain's dog. Two crewmen were still aboard, but at last a line was made fast for the breeches buoy. The first man rescued was brought safely to shore, but the second was knocked down and dragged under by a huge wave as he climbed out of the canvas, and he drowned.
Seaford Gazette, Wednesday 8 February 1989

SEAFORD FROM THE GOLF LINKS

Much excitement prevailed in Seaford on Wednesday, and on that day and on Thursday, multitudes assembled to gaze upon the stranded vessel. Many visitors – some of a very undesirable class – came into the town, and on each day, after the tide had receded, the beach was thronged with spectators, and a sort of marine picnic was held. As for the mariners, both 'ancient' and otherwise, who assembled, their name was legion, while the opinions they expressed were perplexing and bewildering.

Seaford Gazette, 8th February 1899

To the *Peruvian* Figurehead

Behold a pensioner!
Once long ago I sailed the sea,
At the prow of a sailing ship was I,
Bearing the brunt of crested wave,
Fighting the seas when winds were high.
The cargo? Proudly was it borne
Whatever it might be. Our trade
Decreed that our last trip was made;
And wrecked upon this shore she left
Me her dear memory to guard
My fortune has been kind although
I do but grace a promenade,
Dreaming of other scenes and days...

Elizabeth Barrett, Extract from *Ode*, SCM Vol 10, 1936

By dawn on Sunday there was little left of the ship, although for many years the 'ivory nuts' could be found buried amongst the shingle. Local craftsmen created keepsakes of the shipwreck and these found their way into many of the Seaford homes, as the ivory nuts were turned into bottle pourers, and thimble cases. Others were polished smooth and an etching of the ship of the Seven Sisters worked onto the white surface of the shell and sold as souvenirs.

Wendy Hughes, *Shipwrecks of Sussex*

[Examples of these nuts and the restored figurehead of the *Peruvian* can be seen at Seaford Museum]

Tidemills, Bishopston, the boys' Heritage, as most people in Sussex are aware, was the generous gift of the Warren family. It must have given the family great pleasure to hear that Tidemills had rendered valiant service in the great gale of December 6th, when the Dutch ship *Merwede* went ashore close to Tidemills. The nurses there were amongst the first to help with the rocket-line, by means of which the crew of eleven were brought to safety, and to receive hot coffee which put new life into them.

The Gift of Tidemills, SCM January 1930, Vol 4

On Friday 23rd December [1988] the Belgian trawler *White Horse* got into difficulties, ran aground at The Buckle and stuck there for several days, providing an extra point of interest for families out on the traditional post-Christmas-dinner sea-front rambles. There were some dramatic moments when over-strained hawsers, intended to draw the vessel out into deep water, snapped and whipped back towards the spectators. Tugs from Newhaven (with their seasonal fir trees lashed to the masts in time-honoured local manner) eventually pulled her clear.

Patricia Berry, *Seaford Memories 1950–1999*

As you can imagine, with so many ships wrecked at Seaford, most of the wreckage has now become a complete jumble on the seabed, with items from one wreck tangled with another. However there are a group of items that must have come from an as yet unnamed big ship. They sit in line with the last groyne to the east of the Martello tower near to the first two of the Seven Sisters. There is an enormous anchor which has been nicknamed by local divers as 'the Roman Anchor'. It has a 12ft shaft and a ring on the end, approximately 2ft in diameter, with one of the huge iron flukes buried in the seabed. For now, where this ship came from remains a mystery, but it looks large enough to hold a ship that would have been the size of the *HMS Victory*... Between the Martello Tower and Seaford Head divers have also discovered a vast yard – a long spar that supports the head of a square sail. It is 28 ft long and on each end are wheels 5in in diameter for ropes that would have been at least $\frac{1}{2}$in thick and used to swivel the yards. The yard, together with other big timber work, lies at the foot of a large gully running out to sea and is now half-covered in silt. Perhaps one day divers will discover something that will identify this ship.

Wendy Hughes, *Shipwrecks of Sussex*

Smuggling, Looting and Beachcombing

When the River Ouse left Seaford as a 'decayed haven' many of the townspeople, deprived of their livelihood, found less honest ways of earning a living. The whole area was renowned for smuggling, and the celebrated Hawkhurst and Alfriston gangs were frequently in the area... The people of Seaford almost all engaged in such activities. Certainly at one period it was well known that the local Magistrate, as well as the Minister and his three sons, were all accepting bribes from local 'gentlemen'.

Edna and Mac McCarthy, *History Trail of the Town and Cinque Port of Seaford*

When John Rogers captured the smuggler Edward Tomkins at West Chiltington on an August morning in 1732, he must have thought a large reward was his for the taking. Tomkins, a member of the notorious Mayfield Gang, had a price on his head for having tied up a Customs officer during a brandy run on Seaford beach. In fact, Rogers was thrown into gaol for making an unlawful arrest and Tomkins escaped. A determined yet endlessly thwarted bounty hunter, Rogers later managed to round up no fewer than nine smugglers. Magistrates dismissed the charges because none of the men had been caught in the act – and Rogers was whipped for his pains.

David Arscott, *The Sussex Story*

Another report comes to us from a letter dated September 18th, 1783. 'There is a most convenient port, about a mile from Seaford, for smugglers to land their goods, and so daring are they become, that a dozen or more cutters may frequently be seen laying-to in open day. On Tuesday evening, between two and three hundred smugglers on horseback came to Cuckmere, and received various kind of goods from the boats, 'till at last the whole number were laden... About a week before this, upwards of three hundred attended at the same place; and although the sea ran mountains high, the daring men in the cutters made good the landing, to the surprise of everybody, and the men on horseback took all away'.

Edna and Mac McCarthy, *Sussex River*

12th September, 1785. At Bishopstone the sea ran over the full and forced a smuggling boat into the Mill Pond [Tide Mills], and in an instance swept away upwards of 50 chauldron of coal that were on the mill wharf. A man and his horse in crossing the bridge there were forced by the rapidity of the current that overflowed it into the river, but fortunately they were both saved.

SMA (WEA1)

Last Monday morning some smugglers, for reasons best known to themselves, rowed their boats, laden with some 400 caulks of contraband spirits to shore under the battery at Bletchington, where the soldiery soon possessed themselves of the greatest part of her cargo, which they afterwards disposed of to the country people at five shillings a tub, but most of it has, by virtue of search warrants, been recovered by the revenue officers.

Sussex Weekly Advertiser, 8.7.1799

April 1823. Coastguards at Seaford had had warning of a landing of tubs of spirits in the early hours and when the suspect craft came in sight they carefully tracked it until they were able to make certain that there could be no escape. They boarded the boat and found twenty tubs under tarpaulins. After unloading the tubs and ensuring that the crew was under guard, they tapped the barrels to find that each of them contained nothing more than sea water. While they had been attending to the decoy boat 300 tubs of spirits had been unloaded not half a mile away at Newhaven Tidemills and made off with up-country.

WH Johnson, *A Grim Almanack of Sussex*

The most serious drawback to Seaford is the civility on the part of the real 'natives'. This last named characteristic is reputed to be due to the lawless wrecking spirit which survives to the present day, derived from former generations of inhabitants, notorious wreckers and smugglers, plus the corruption of morals induced by men's votes having been worth £1000. There is still discernible among the people of Seaford a mixture of cringing servility and vulgar bullying...
George F Chambers, *Tourist's Guide to the County of Sussex*, 1891

But of course smuggling is a thing of the past. Or is it? In recent years an abortive attempt was made to smuggle Asian immigrants ashore at Cuckmere Haven. Possibly other attempts have been successful.
Edna and Mac McCarthy, *Sussex River*, 1975

Looting and Beachcombing

In 1544, Henry VIII granted Seaford a Charter reaffirming its rights, duties and privileges as a Cinque Port, even though it had ceased to be a port. The townspeople, deprived of their livelihood by the new haven, used the Charter for their own ends. Their rights to flotsam and jetsam were exploited to the full, even to the extent of wrecking ships to create pickings for themselves. These Seaford wreckers were well-known and nicknamed 'Shags' or 'Cormorants'.
Marie Lewis, *A Brief History of Seaford*

An examination of John Baker took place on 22nd May, 1633, before Dr Thomas Rivers, as to a ship cast away or found on shore at Seaford, on a Sunday in January then last. Baker having heard thereof at almost sunset, put his sheep in fold, and went down to the ship... He had out of a room in the hinder-part of the ship a scarlet or red cloak, lined with stuff like velvet, of the same colour; also a pair of knee-tops of cloth, lined with red taffeta; one silk garter; a piece of cloth lined with black taffeta, and fringed with black silk, about a yard square; and one glove, wrought with silver; all which he carried to his own home...
MA Lower & WD Cooper, *Further Memorials of Seaford*, 1865

As late as 1809, when on 7th December seven ships were stranded in Seaford Bay, the people of the Downs and neighbourhood flocked to the shore for plunder, 'and,' says an 'Eye-Witness', who published a pamphlet on the event, 'horror rivets my heart as I write it, among the humane and feeling many, there were still those monsters of rapine to be found, who regardless of the fates of the tempest-beaten seamen, untouched by the agonized shrieks of the exhausted and the dying, were intent on plunder only; nor could the ghastly corps that, at intervals, the tide cast between them and the objects they were grasping at, for an instant suspend their horrible and infamous purpose. To these wretches 'conscience will some day speak loudly'; the punishment of guilt, though delayed, is certain; and miscreants, such as are above alluded to, Heaven will never suffer with impunity to escape.'

Arthur Beckett, *The Spirit of the Downs*, 1949

Dec 1815. The *Adamant*, out of Malta and carrying an extremely valuable cargo, struggled for hours up the Channel. Huge seas and powerful winds made her progress slow. The hope was that she might make Newhaven but midnight came and passed and the port was still some distance away. In the next few hours, the vessel foundered on the rocks near enough for the townsfolk, undeterred by the continuing storm, to come out to help themselves to whatever they could. And the word was about - had been for hours – so that men and women from all around the district turned up with baskets and sacks and wagons, seeking their share. But in London, in Lloyd's Coffee House, the underwriters – when they heard of their loss, estimated at £100,000 – determined that something must be done to stop the regular wholesale plunder of wrecks. They sent men from the Bow Street office down to Sussex with orders to pursue the matter rigorously. Armed with writs the 'Runners' entered as many as 200 houses. In Horsham and at the Pelham Arms in Seaford they found sheets of copper. Elsewhere, in Blatchington, Alfriston, Bishopstone and Newhaven, they found more evidence of plunder. Some people, learning of the effectiveness of the search, suddenly recalled that they had property from the *Adamant* and informed the officers.

WH Johnson, *A Grim Almanack of Sussex*

[Some contemprary press reports stated that opium was found under the copper]

Diary: Monday, 4th February 1884

There has been quite an aspect along the coast – two large ships *The City of Lucknow* and *Simla* were in collision when the latter sank (crew saved) and from Dover to Brighton all kinds of things were washed ashore, pianos, dead pigs, [?] etc but the worst part is that 32 gallon casks of spirit and beer came ashore in large numbers and people flock to the sea shore to get drunk. One of Uncle George's men, a carter, drank and made himself ill. Was taken to Brighton hospital and died in a few hours. It is reported that 6 men have died from drink at Newhaven. Among the navvies there has been much trouble and we heard that they have all been sent off by special train to be out of the way of temptation. The doctors had to telegraph to Lewes for more stomach pumps they had not enough. The coastguards stave in the tops of all barrels and empty the brandy on the beach but in spite of this precaution many contrive to get enough to get fearfully drunk. Extra men are put on to help the coastguards and people are forbidden to go on the beach.

Diary of Ruth Caroline Morris née Verral, ESRO AMS 6572/6/1

We have been flanked by planks of timber all along our shores, the Cuckmere Valley has another foe to contend with; since this ship [*Ice Prince*] relieved itself of its cargo planks have been sighted as far east as Dungeness…

A policy of action to deal with this and any future disaster of this magnitude must be addressed to avoid confusion, chaos, and misunderstanding to whether this is salvage or not. How do you define jetsam, flotsam, salvage, shipwreck cargo on this scale to your local beachcomber?

Seaford Town Council *Newsletter*, Issue 19, April 2008

Heroism at Sea

The *Weymouth* [wrecked in 1809] had a crew of ten but only four reached shore. The hero of the rescue was Mr Ginn of Lewes Barrack Department who, at great personal risk, led the rescue and managed to drag the four to safety, including the cabin boy clutching the master's pet raccoon in his arms. He was determined to save the animal as he was so grateful for the kindness shown to him by the master, who on board divided his favours between him and the raccoon.

Wendy Hughes, *Shipwrecks of Sussex*

Anstruther's wife and children, however, could not escape in this manner. They were rescued by two men whose enormous courage was apparently matched by their undoubted strength. They rowed out to *Harlequin*, succeeded in clambering aboard, tied the children to their backs and brought them down to the rowing boat. The mother was then able to join them although how she came down to safety is not recorded.

Throughout the morning there were several such acts of courage. The sole survivor of *Midbedacht* was saved by Lieutenant Derenzy and men of the 81st Foot from nearby Blatchington barracks. The officer waded into the sea and grabbed the drowning mariner by the hair. The tug of the waves then dragged both men back towards the open water. Another soldier dived in to their rescue. He, too, was soon in difficulty. All three were ultimately saved by a line of soldiers who reached out into the sea to effect the rescue. Such chains of men saved other strugglers in the raging waters that morning.

WH Johnson, *Sussex Disasters*

Some of the older Seafordians no doubt still remember Richard Mallett [coastguard], and the heroic deed he did on December 16th, 1869. On this day a terrific gale raged in Seaford Bay, and a French vessel was driven ashore close to the Martello Tower. Mallett fastened a line round his waist and swam out through the surf, establishing, at the risk of his life, communication with the vessel, which was fast becoming a wreck. By this means he was instrumental in saving the whole of the crew, with one exception, a boy who unfortunately was washed off the deck and not recovered. For this heroic action he was publicly presented at the Town Hall with a valuable gold watch and chain, and a purse of money... The total subscriptions amounted to £26 14s. 4½d, the odd halfpenny being indicative of the general character of the subscriptions.

WR Wynter, *Old Seaford*, 1922

Never forgotten in those parts was the night in November 1943 when the crew of the Newhaven lifeboat made gallant attempts in appalling conditions, heavy seas and a full southwest gale – at great cost to themselves, including the loss of their signalman and serious injury to several others – to help the 25 men on board the stricken HM trawler *Avanturine*.

Patricia Berry, *Seaford Memories 1950–1999*

Sea Defences

Had proper piers been erected at Seaford cliff, and had groins been placed on that bar of beach which must have extended across the bay to the south-west, far beyond the present boundary of the land, Seaford would not have lost its harbour; nor would it have been compelled, as it has recently been from its want of population and importance, 'to hide its diminished head'. From the want of these defences, we find that the harbour has been obliterated, the ancient bed of the river nearly filled up, and the beach rolled back upon the land, so as considerably to encroach upon its limits. Unless this progress be stopped by some mechanical power, directed by the still more mighty intellect of man, it must still go on.
TW Horsfield, *The History of Sussex*, 1835

On the 1st day of May, 1881, the first spadeful of concrete was thrown into the trench for the formation of the new sea-wall, and in November following it was completed. The length from the East Cliff to the western end is 3,230 feet; the height of the wall together with that of the slope of the Parade gives a margin of safety of five feet above the greatest known height ever reached by a flood wave at Seaford.
W Banks, *Seaford: Past and Present*, 1892

Talking Cat – Wendy, claimed to be Britain's only talking cat, has died at Seaford, Sussex. She once made a recording for a programme on the Seaford sea defences and surprised everybody by saying in rhythmic tones: 'What, no sea wall, chum?'
Hull Daily Mail, 20.6.1947

A major cause for concern was the state of the sea-wall; little maintenance had been possible during the war years, the beach having been closed off with tank-traps, barbed-wire entanglements and other anti-invasion devices. A four-day storm in October 1945 and another two months later did extensive damage. In the latter, four large sections of wall collapsed, two of them more than 200 feet long. Expert advice was sought most urgently, resulting in proposals for a £10,000 improvement scheme, but this came too late to prevent flooding in the lower part of the town in 1949, and was only the beginning of problems for our city fathers.
Patricia Berry, *Seaford Memories 1950–1999*

The work began in January 1987 and the transformation of the beach was dramatic. Massive granite rocks quarried in Spain, arrived at Newhaven Harbour and were brought to the bay by road. On top of this, shingle sucked up from Ower's Bank off the coast of Bognor Regis, was deposited at a rate of one ton per second.

The work was completed on time and just in time too! Just two weeks after completion, on October 16, 1987 the Great Hurricane struck and the new beach surely saved the town from disaster

It is interesting to read some of the information which was given by the contractors when they were bidding for the work. It was suggested that the beach would be 'maintenance free' and loved by residents and especially children.

I am not sure that this is the case as every January huge diggers and bulldozers have to relocate the shingle at a cost of millions of pounds and some residents, particularly the elderly, complain that the beach is too steep for them to reach the shoreline.
Kevin Gordon, *From A Seaford Album*, Sussex Express, 17.07.09

THE LAW, CRIME AND PUNISHMENT

The Town Hall

First, of course, must come the town hall, ridiculously small to us in 1974 with a population of 16,000 but quite adequate for the business of that day. All the town's business, except the actual election of the bailiff, took place here, the courts, the elections and every other civic function. It has become fashionable now to laugh at the pomp and ceremony of the eighteenth century carried on in every small village with the utmost seriousness, no less than the great Charles Dickens himself poked fun at Seaford's town hall because the bailiff's chair was merely a bench placed against a wall which bore a painted replica of the chair back.

Joan A Astell, *To the Independent Electors of Seaford, 1768–1786*

The Police

In the old days, previous to the present coastguards, there existed a body of men known as the Preventive Force, whose principal duty was in the prevention of contraband goods being landed on the coast. According to records, they sometimes had quite an exciting time, and many were the fights which ensued between them and the smugglers. The following is interesting on account of its being composed of local men who served in this force in 1789:

Thomas Baker, aged 39, of Seaford, riding officer, strong able officer, and makes many seizures;

Joseph Stevens, aged 63, of Seaford, commander of the Seaford boat;

Gabriel Brooker, aged 64, of Newhaven, landing waiter, acts also as collector's clerk, but being very corpulent, is not so active as formerly...

WR Wynter, *Old Seaford* 1922

May 1856
Application for situation in Police Force
8 Claremont Place Hastings
Perceiving that four men is required from the Borough of Hastings Police I beg to offer myself as a candidate. My height is 5'6¾" aged 34 – married, never previously employed in any other Police, have served under government nearly 20 years as Mail driver from Lewes to Seaford and the last half of that time also acted as Postmaster at Seaford left in consequence of so small a salary and in order to allow my sister to succeed me. For the last two months was employed in the Coast Guard service and in consequence of the return of the men from the Crimea was dismissed. If you should think to elect me I can assure you that no effort should be spared in my part to discharge the duties of the office faithfully...
James Rusbridge
ESRO dhbe/DH/B/136/709

The very first authorised uniform for the Constabulary was a top hat, frock coat and trousers of heavy melton type texture. A constable was permitted to carry a cutlass if he could induce two Justices of the Peace, living in his neighbourhood, to certify that his beat was especially dangerous. There is no record of cutlasses ever having been used.

The top hat was discontinued in 1864 and replaced by a short lived 'bowler' type helmet. Earlier issues bore the numerals on the front, later they were transferred to the collar and worn in that position until early 1953. Boots were shapeless and could be worn on either foot. Constables were recommended to wear them on different feet each day and never to wash their feet but to rub them each evening with sweet oil.

Records show that in 1885 a narrow type helmet was introduced on which the present day pattern is founded. Black leggings were worn and walking sticks were permitted to be carried, though it was necessary to remind constables that this concession did not include umbrellas.

East Sussex Police 1840–1967, SMA (LO)

In 1890 pedal cycles were introduced into the force and instructions stated that no man over 18 stone would be permitted to ride them... At the outbreak of War – 1939 – and during the war until its cessation in 1945, some hundreds of soldiers were billeted in the town, Canadians, Americans and English Regiments, who were billeted at the large private schools and the large numbers of other empty properties in the town. The Canadians especially gave me a great deal of trouble from a criminal point of view, as they all liked their intoxicating liquor to a large degree and they used to break into lock up licensed premises, steal spirits and other liquor, then return to their billets and help themselves when they required it.

Autobiography – Charles White – Local Detective, SMA (LO)

Court Cases and Records

Extracts from the Old Records in the Town Chest of the Town and Port of Seaford:

1577. The Jury presented Joan à Wood for being a witch and sentenced her to be placed in the pillory. The site of the pillory was in front of the inn now known as the 'Old Tree', and was standing in this year.

1579. The servants of Mr Thomas Elphicke, bailiff, are presented by the Jury for throwing a dead dog into the highway, also those of his kinsman, Hugh Elphicke, for committing a like offence with dead hogs. Fined two pence each.

1582. The jury present John Browne, butcher, for selling unwholesome meat. He was fined VId [sixpence].
...The Bailiff charges John Comber, and all in court, if they know of 'person or persons within this township that foyster, ayde, vitell, maynteyne, or succor any thieves or pyrates' to declare the truth thereupon at their peril.

1595. That Gilbert Duplake has exposed flesh for sale during the time of Lent.

1620. They present 'Cooper's wife, for makinge discord betwixt neibours.'

1711. December 7th. The Barbers of the Corporation of Seaford were each fined 2s 6d for shaving on the Sabbath Day.

WR Wynter, *Old Seaford*

11 Nov 1628. John Willett, for his irreverent behaviour in the church as sitting with his hat on his head in tyme of divine service; as also for his rude and disorderly behaviour as throwing stones at others that sit in the chancel in tyme of divine service and sermon to the disturbing of the minister and the rest of the congregation; as also for fighting in the churchyard, and for a very negligent comer to the Church on the Sabboth day.

Rodney Castleden, *On Blatchington Hill, History of a Downland Village*

Theft, Prison and Mock Marriage

The Information and Complaint of Hannah, Wife of John Smith made on oath before us Thomas Chambers and Thomas Harben Esquires, two of his Majesty's Justices of the Peace, in and for the said Town and Port, the third day of May Eighteen Hundred, that on or about the fourteenth day of April last, divers goods, the property of the said John Smith, to wit four child's pieces and one child's bed, of the value of about three shillings have feloniously been stolen, taken and carried away from a field near his dwelling house belonging to Thomas Chambers Esquire at Seaford aforesaid; and that she hath just cause to suspect and doth suspect that Ann Hughes the wife of Richard Hughes, Mariner, of the Town and Port aforesaid, did steal, take and carry away the same, the property above stated being found in her profession.

And, therefore she, the said Hannah Smith, on the part of her Husband, prayeth that justice may be done...

ESRO SEA/73

The Request of Samuel Potter now Confined in the Prison of the said Town and Port, To the Bailiff of the said Place,

To wit,

Sheweth

That your said Petitioner most earnestly Prays that by reason of the said Prison being very Damp and for several other causes wish[es] to be removed from the said Prison to take his Trial at the next Assizes for the County of Sussex, to be held at East Grinstead on Monday the thirteenth Instant and if your said Petitioner can have his Request granted he will readily pay all charges incurred touching and concerning his being removed as abovesaid and it will be considered as a particular favor granted, to your very humble Servant, the mark X of Samuel Potter

ESRO SEA/126 8 March 1797

[Potter was sentenced to 7 years transportation]

23rd August 1912. Lewes Police Court. Case of mock marriage at Seaford. A patient at Surrey Convalescent Home and a lady worker there were falsely married at 16 East Street, Seaford, by a person who was neither priest or registrar – reason to obtain money by 'so called registrar' who obtained the couple's signature on promissory notes saying they were marriage certificates. Couple parted after marriage but the registrar? tried to obtain payment of promissory note from the groom? at Wellington Hotel. Groom and registrar on bail.

13th December 1912. Assizes trial of mock marriage. Registrar 10 months hard labour and Groom 6 months hard labour.

Sussex Express

Fights

Last Friday morning a duel was fought on the beach near Bletchington Barracks between Captain D.....n and Lieutenant L.....n of the second battalion of the Derbyshire militia in which the former was shot in the abdomen... Not having been able to learn from any good authority the particulars of the dispute which gave rise to this unhappy affair, we for the present decline saying anything further on the subject.

Sussex Weekly Advertiser, 11th March 1799

We are glad to hear that Captain D, who was shot by Lieutenant L in the duel stated in our last, continues in a promising way and that the most flattering hopes are now entertained for his speedy recovery. The meeting, we understand, took place in consequence of something said by Captain D on the subject of a matrimonial connection which principally concerned Lieutenant L and which he considered as disrespectful. The Captain fired first, and directed his pistol so skilfully that the ball grazed the forehead of Mr L, who then fired and wounded his antagonist, as before stated. Captain D (who has a wife and five children) on finding himself wounded, asked Mr L if he had received the satisfaction he required, who answered in the affirmative, when both parties retired with their seconds who were officers of the same regiment. The peril in which the challenger had placed his adversary's life, rendered it prudent for him to absent himself, and the two seconds, also fearing the consequences, followed his example.

Sussex Weekly Advertiser, 18 March 1799

Trouble at Seaford: (Mar 31st 1800) T Harben Esq, the Bailiff of Seaford, having between eleven and twelve o'clock on last Thursday night, received information that Lieutenant T ___ and J O____e Esq were to meet at six the next morning on the beach, near the Signal-post, for the purpose of fighting a duel, ordered the Constable to take the parties immediately into custody who in consequence caused Mr O to be called from his bed, and made a prisoner of him: but the Lieutenant, to elude his search, concealed himself the whole night in a bathing machine, and in the morning, attended with his second at the time and place appointed, where he waited two hours for the arrival of his antagonist, and then retired to his apartment in the barrack, where he was also taken into custody. They were, however, soon after liberated, on finding two sureties, who entered into recognizances of £150 each, for their keeping the peace towards each other in future. The challenge, we understand, arose from a dispute between the parties, touching the priority of claim to [a] certain young lady in the neighbourhood.

SMA (LO)

Bribery and Political Chicanery

The Duke's [of Newcastle] erstwhile protégé, William Gage of Firle Place, had recently crossed into the Tory camp. So while he and his father, Lord Gage, were determined that William should continue to represent Seaford, Newcastle would have none of it and nominated William Pitt and the sitting member, William Hay.

On the eve of the election [1747] a feast was prepared at Bishopstone Place where the Pelham family entertained William Pitt and all the local gentry and influential farmers until daybreak when they were all taken in carriages to the old town hall to vote.
John Odam, *The Seaford Story, 1000–2000 AD*

The Treasury patronage was afterwards transferred from him [Mr Harison] to Mr Harben, who, on pretence of being Mr Harison's friend, obtained from him the purchase of some acres of his estate within the borough, at a very cheap rate, and having built a house, he gradually unfolded as deep a piece of treachery as was ever shown. He procured creatures of his own to be elected bailiff and freemen, and then procured the dismissal of Mr Harison from his appointments, which he divided among his own associates, and not at all neglecting his own interest, obtained the appointment of Receiver-General of Stamp Duties for Sussex, worth £600 per annum, for his son, and other advantages; and immediately afterwards a system of the greatest profligacy was commenced, strenuously opposed by the independent Mr James Hurdis, who yet lives in the grateful recollection of many of the old inhabitants of Seaford.
TW Horsfield, *The History of Sussex*, Appendix, *Parliamentary History*, 1835

The subsequent history of Seaford presents us with few incidents of interest. After the restitution to it of electoral rights in the 17th century, it became one of the most corrupt of 'rotten boroughs', and thus almost inevitably, the tone of morals became low, while the material prosperity of the place was gradually deteriorated.
MA Lower, *Notes on Seaford*, 1868

In the 'good' old times, bribery and corruption were rampant at the elections ... Not many years ago, the writer well remembers a house in Church Street which had been built by a prospective candidate in order to secure one vote. Another elector told his candidate that he was not fit to go to the polling booth, as his clothes were too shabby; he got a new suit.

Another tale is told of a candidate who in order to secure a majority made three or four electors right royally drunk, and then locked them up in a shed, but the affair leaking out just before the conclusion of the election, they were rescued by the rival candidate and taken in a more or less fuddled condition to the booth, where they duly recorded their votes.

WR Wynter, *Old Seaford*, 1922

To the credit of the people of Seaford it should be told that even in these depressing times, when liberty of voting was practically unknown, they put up from time to time brave fights for their liberty, which invariably failed. The House, before whom their petitions came, was in those days too much under the influence of those who wished to retain control of the voting system to grant much license to electors.

It must surely be some consolation to those who deplore the shackling of its political life which Seaford endured for such a length of time, to know that the old borough was the instrument of bringing into the forefront of the nation's life several illustrious men who, by their varied talents, have done notable service to their country.

The Rev GP Crawford, *Seaford in Parliament 1660–1832*, SCM Vol 5 1931

The matter of voting entitlement also sparked off occasional trouble in the election of the bailiff. Two cases were taken to the high court in 1763 and 1764 involving the elections of Robert Stone and Thomas Washer, when the populace claimed that they had not been properly represented. In 1775 in an attempt to displace the bailiff, Lancelot Harison, the court house was invaded, a shoemaker took away the town chest with its records and there was almost a reading of the Riot Act before order was restored. In 1789 there was another riot at the town hall inspired by THB Oldfield, a political reformer, no doubt with an eye to the main chance.

John Odam, *Bygone Seaford*

Espionage, Rape, Mutiny, Arson and Murder

Yesterday, as a man named Green, belonging to Seaford, was traversing the beach of that place, he observed floating near the shore a cask, rendered conspicuous by a flag, which he secured and took home. This little vessel had, no doubt, been launched by order of Bonaparte from the French coast to convey information to this country as the cargo consisted of two packets with French super-scriptions in print. They were delivered to the Rev Mr Evans, who immediately transmitted them to Mr Leach in London (unopened) in order that he might forward them to the Government. They probably contained the 29th and 30th Bulletins, as they have since been published in the London papers. The cask, which was somewhat larger than a half-anker [about 18 litres], was admirably constructed for the purpose. The flagstaff was secured by being tightly driven into the bung-hole, which was cemented round with a composition quite impervious to water, and to the bottom was affixed a bag containing two shots to give it a proper degree of buoyancy. It is now in possession of Major Grant of this town.
London Globe, February 6th, 1808

Rape

Arthur Cleveland, John Moynihan, and Cornelius Moynihan were charged with rape. Mr Willoughby prosecuted; the prisoners were not defended by counsel. The three prisoners in this case were Artillerymen, stationed at Newhaven. The prosecutrix resides at Seaford. One Sunday evening in February last she was walking from Seaford to Newhaven in company with a man named Hoadley, a mate of one of the Newhaven steamers. Hoadley had gone into a public house called the Buckle, at Bishopstone, about half-way be-tween Newhaven and Seaford, and the prosecutrix, who has lost one of her feet, was sitting outside on a form, waiting for him, when, according to the evidence for the prosecution, the three prisoners seized her, dragged her to an adjoining piece of open ground, and, notwithstanding the resistance of the prosecutrix and the attempts of Hoadley and a fourth soldier to protect her, they each committed the offence with which they were charged. The only one of the prisoners who stated anything in his defence was Cleveland, who

said that he was so drunk that he did not recollect what had happened. THE LORD CHIEF JUSTICE, in passing sentence, commented upon the atrocious circumstances of the offence which three strong men had contrived to perpetrate against a weak and defenceless woman, who had given them no encouragement by levity or impropriety. He must pass a severe sentence, which would serve as a warning against the idle and silly belief that intoxication could afford any defence or palliation for such conduct. The prisoners were sentenced to 15 years penal servitude.
The Times, 22.3.1875

Mutiny

On Friday, April 17 [1795] some five hundred members of the Oxford Militia mutinied, marching from their barracks at Blatchington, near Seaford, with fixed bayonets. It had been a hard winter, and a sharp rise in bread prices had provoked riots throughout the country: indeed, members of the same militia had recently been jailed for raiding bakers' shops in Chichester, only to be freed by a violent mob. Now they marched first to Seaford, where they seized quantities of flour, bread and meat and sold them to local people at less than the going rate; next to the tide mill near Bishopstone, where they forced the crew of a sloop loading flour to sail their cargo to Newhaven; and finally to Newhaven itself, where they took possession of the town and sold the commandeered flour at what they regarded as a fair price.

The severity of the punishment inflicted upon their ringleaders was predictable ...Two of the militiamen, privates James Sykes and William Sampson, were hanged at Horsham. Two others, privates Edward Coke and Henry Parish, were shot by a firing squad at Goldstone Bottom in Brighton...
David Arscott, *The Sussex Story*

Arson

The proposal to introduce the Poor Law Amendment Act of 1834 with its much misunderstood regulations for Unions and New Workhouses sparked off sporadic disturbances over much of England. In Sussex, these were scattered, but Seaford became involved in them... On May 14th the great medieval barn at Chinton [Chyngton] farm, owned by Lord Chichester and tenanted by Chambers, both supporters of Poor Law reform, was set on fire but the blaze was extinguished before much damage was done. On the 16th, two large barns on Sutton farm, owned by Harrison, were fired; they were saved although two pigs were lost in the flames. Three men were arrested for this arson, a traditional form of protest, but released on a lack of evidence.

An Embryonic Brighton? Victorian and Edwardian Seaford, ed. John Lowerson

Murder

24th September 1934. The body of a man washed up on the beach at Seaford was missing its head and legs. Over each collarbone was a surgical incision made most probably by a doctor. So delicate was the work that it could not have been done by an amateur. Beneath the left incision was a pad of cotton wool: in the right incision a piece of silk had been tied round a blood vessel. It was believed that the man was dead before the incisions were made and before he went into the sea. It was estimated that the body had been in the sea for at least two months, most likely after being thrown overboard from a ship.

SMA (LO)

SEAFORD FROM SPLASH POINT. 054.

WAR, DISEASE, HEALTHCARE AND DEATH

Military Matters

As a proof of the decay of the Port of Seaford so far back as the time of Queen Elizabeth, we find that the guns which had evidently been used for the defence of the entrance to the harbour were stowed away in a barn, as the following record will show:

1576, 18th Elizabeth, November 6th. The Bailiff, Jurat, and Commonalty demised to Henrie Becke for ten years 'One Barne standing by the Haven in Seaforde except so much rome as the Gonnes shall occupie in the lower rome of the said barne' for the sum of twelve pence a year.

RW Wynter, *Old Seaford*, 1922

Battle

[The Battle of the Buckle in 1545 fought on the beach against the invading French by Sir Nicholas Pelham]

HIS BRAVE EXPLOIT IN GREAT KING HENRY'S DAYES
AMONG THE WORTHYE HATH A WORTHIER TOMBE:
WHAT TIME THE FRENCH SOUGHT TO HAVE SACKT SEAFOORD,
THIS PELHAM DID REPEL THEM BACK ABOORD

Punning epitaph of Sir Nicholas Pelham, d. 1559, in St Michael's Church, Lewes

Batteries

All that now remains of a battery built in AD 1762 between where the Esplanade Hotel now stands and the sea, and which was in existence thirty years ago, are a few pieces of brick and concrete work embedded in the shingle before the sea wall there.

...The other, called the 'Blatchington Battery', from its being in that parish, was built at the same time as the former – but originally only extended half way down the then existing slope from the top of the cliff – leaving a grassy bank between its face and the shingle. Forty years ago, in view of the encroachments of the sea, it was extended to a point marked by a bit of masonry which remains in situ on the beach and faced in a line with it to a level with the cliff with Purfleet stone. It mounted four sixty-eight and two thirty-two pounders... All that is now left of it are the few fragments of masonry and blocks of stone lying on the narrow strip of shingle under the cliff against which they were built.

Descriptive Guide to Seaford, Newhaven & Vicinity, 189?

Seaford Barracks

Last week a prostitute who had been too lavish with her favours to the soldiery was removed from Bletchington Barracks to the House of Correction in this Town.

Sussex Weekly Advertiser, 6.4.1795

A bowel complaint has of late been very rife here and in many instances proved fatal. Upwards of thirty children belonging to soldiers in our barracks, have been carried off by it in a short space of time.

Sussex Weekly Advertiser, 7.9.1807

There never was a place so ruined as when it was visited for a week this summer by a strong force of the Honourable Artillery Company – noisy and bibulous warriors, who stalked about the village as if they had bought Sussex... who scared quiet visitors with camp songs, and played at soldiering, it must be said, neither wisely nor well.

SMA, press cutting, 1878

World War I

The chief features of the place were the two great camps on the outskirts of the town, the 'South Camp' for the Canadians, and the 'North Camp' for the 'Imperials' as they were called locally.

A few days after my arrival, however, the rivalry and jealousy came to a crisis between the two sets of men when a hot-headed Canadian 'Tommy', resenting a reprimand from an 'Imperial' NCO, assaulted and injured him so badly that he died the following day. I believe that it was never allowed to get into the newspapers, but it was this unfortunate affair which finally decided 'The Authorities' to remove the 'Imperials' to Shorncliffe and reserve both the Seaford camps for Canadians only.

...Though many of them were British born, they all belonged to the Canadian Army ...Quite a large number were Scottish 'kilties', some of them really magnificent men – huge, fine fellows well over six feet high, with their bonnets tipped jauntily on one side, and their curled cock's feathers looking quite aggressive; others so delicate and undeveloped that it was a wonder they had passed the medical tests.

Agnes H Carter, *A Canteen in a Canadian Camp* (1917), SCM Vol 8 1934

After the quiet West Indians left, the Canadians arrived. Literally thousands of them. Again many of them worshipped at St Leonard's and when they left, they gave the church two brass maple leafs which were fixed to the front pews where they sat. Towards the end of the war many of the Canadians died during the Flu epidemic and nearly 200 are buried at the cemetery.

Kevin Gordon, St Leonard's & St Luke's Churches, Seaford *Magazine*, Mar/Apr 2011

Almost immediately the submarine crew spotted the aircraft and there was a desperate scramble to submerge. The seaplane observer stood up behind his pilot with a hand placed on his head. The pilot's head was lightly moved right or left according to the direction required, while he concentrated on maintaining level flight at a constant height.

Lt Ackery felt a slight bump as Lt Dangerfield let loose the 112 pounder and he was able to look over the side and see the bomb hit the water six feet from the hull of the submarine. It was a near miss. There was a great force of water, and the submarine disappeared under the water, but shortly afterwards, oil appeared to come to the surface.

The aircrew sent a signal to base, then continued circling until their fuel was low. It just did not occur to them to drop their other bomb! Arriving back at Newhaven, the crew received a hero's welcome, it being the first occasion that 242 squadron had attacked a submarine. Unfortunately they were not credited with a 'kill', which would have meant a financial bonus.

Peter Fellows, *A Short History of a local Seaplane Station 1917–1920*

Witness at Inquest on death of Joseph Plant Wild shot by Stanko Jovan Layovich, The British Columbia Regimental Depot, Seaford:

Stanko Layovich being duly sworn states: 'I shot Pte Wild because he made a statement that he made a woman of me. He said that he had committed sodomy with me for threepence. Wild has made that statement to the officers and other ranks, and that is the reason I was was not given the decorations for which I was recommended; because he spread that lie I shot him. I shot him with full consciousness for the sake of military honour. For dishonour of that kind I would shoot my own father.'

Coroner's Report 14th August 1917, ESRO COR/1/3/558

[Layovich was sentenced to imprisonment by a civil court. Wild is buried at Seaford Cemetery]

The news of the Armistice on 11.11.18 came from a light aircraft which had landed in Seaford from France, there being no radio in those days. We heard of it at about 12.30 pm from some Canadian troops nearby. The flagstaff, whose halliards had rotted away during the war, was pulled down by the soldiers and boys, and fresh halliards made so that the occasion could be properly marked with flags flying.

St Peter's School Magazine, vol. III, 1974, SMA (Schools)

World War II

Seaford was one of the seaside towns which suffered considerably by enemy action, but owing to the evacuation scheme the casualties were not nearly so numerous as would otherwise have been the case. Twenty-two properties were totally destroyed, including a number in the centre of the town, 54 were found to be beyond repair and were demolished, 82 were severely damaged but were capable of repair, and 1,944 were slightly damaged. There were 1,053 alerts and 42 incidents. The number of high-explosive bombs dropped was 142, with five oil bombs, while approximately 10,000 incendiaries were scattered over the district. Two bombs of other types were also dropped, one enemy aircraft crashed near the town, and there were four machine-gunning and cannon-fire incidents...

ALARMING INCIDENT – On April lst 1941, at about 7.35 pm, another lone raider damaged a part of the shopping centre. It flew over Broad Street, Church Street, West Street and Chatham Place, dropping three high explosive bombs. One destroyed the old manor House in Broad Street, another went through Turrell's garage close by and pierced the brick wall at the western end of the building. It then shot across the parish churchyard, taking pieces off tombstones in its flight, and finally came to rest, unexploded, just outside the back door of the Plough Inn. The landlord's wife had been frightened by the raid, and her husband, in trying to assure her that all the danger was over, took her outside to prove it, only to find a large bomb lying close to his door-step...

SEAFORD COULD TAKE IT – Despite the trials and tribulations which the people at Seaford had to contend with, splendid work was done by all the ARP services, and although there were many grim incidents, there were also a number of humorous ones.

On one occasion, a party of wardens had to get out on duty in double quick time, and ran to their post wearing only their pyjamas. Their Chief Warden, Mr E J Gretton (an old soldier of the last war), was equal to the occasion, however, and, lining them up, calmly asked them why they were unshaven.

The War in East Sussex 1945, Sussex Express

...the whole of this area became a 'sealed off' zone. Many civilians were evacuated, and check points around the whole area assured that no unauthorised person entered or left. Some civilians remained, but their relatives and friends from outside the area were not allowed to visit them.

Some shops, such as Sainsbury's, closed down completely for the duration of the war, and, after the Dunkirk evacuation, this area hourly awaited invasion. Troops, many of them Canadian, poured into Seaford and other properties. Beach defences were erected, mines and booby traps were set, guns were sited and all stood on alert. It has since been revealed that, in his 'Operation Sea Lion', his plans for the invasion of Britain, Hitler planned landings in this area with the capture of Newhaven Harbour as an urgent priority. But the Germans failed to gain the control of the skies which was the necessary prelude to invasion, and many of those air battles were fought out over Sussex.

Edna and Mac McCarthy, *History Trail of the Town and Cinque Port of Seaford*

Early in World War II, the villagers [Tide Mills] had a lucky escape. Being sited along a vulnerable beach area, they were given 24 hours' notice to evacuate. Soon afterwards many bombs fell in the immediate area. But anything that remained of the village was not to survive long.

In July 1940, sappers moved in to use the area as a training ground for street fighting. The buildings were eventually destroyed – a measure also necessary to ensure that the houses could not be used in the event of a German invasion.

Today only the ghosts of the past can be found among the derelict buildings – in what was once a thriving community.

Leslie Oppitz, c 1988, SMA (local press scrapbook)

As a Territorial Company Royal Engineers we were mobilised at Seaford, Sussex, a week before war was declared and of course we still slept at home. However, once war was declared we were paid billeting allowance of the magnificent sum of ten pence, old money, per night. The married chaps thought this was a great joke, being paid all this just to sleep with their wives.

On the very first Sunday of the war we had a Church Parade service at our local church. This was taken by the Vicar the Revd Charles Maxwell. After his sermon he started to walk down the steps of the pulpit, stopped halfway, paused for a moment then returned to the pulpit. There was a deep silence as everybody wondered what was coming, and even two years later in the desert in North Africa, I had chaps that never went to Church say to me, what a first-class man your Vicar was, we have never forgotten what he said. I shall never forget either.

He faced us for a moment in silence then said, 'War brings out the best or the worst in a man, but remember the choice is always your own.'

Ted Pettit, *A Sapper Goes to War or More Lives than a Cat*, SMA (AF5)

At one time the Nazis attempted to snuff out football in Seaford. On 18 November 1940 the clubhouse at The Crouch received a direct hit from one of three attacking warplanes. What the building looked like then (before it was bombed) is now unknown, but it evidently had the appearance of something with militarily strategic significance.

Seaford Town Football Club http://www.stfc.org.uk/aboutl.htm

Lieut.-Col. GCT Keyes, VC, MC

In November he was in command of the raiding party which attacked General Rommel's headquarters in Libya...

...Without guides, in dangerous and precipitous country, faced with a climb of over 1,800 ft in pitch darkness and an approach march of 18 miles which they knew must culminate in an attack on the German Headquarters, soaked to the skin by continuous torrential rain and shivering with cold from half a gale of wind, the fast ebbing morale of the detachment was maintained solely by Colonel Keyes' stolid determination and magnetic powers of leadership...

King's Mead Terminal Letters, summer term 1942. SMA (Schools).

[A pupil from 1926–31. He had stormed Rommel's private quarters before he was shot.]

Falklands War 1982

Lieut.-Col. Herbert Jones, VC, OBE

Col H's storming of the enemy trench changed the course of the conflict, and he was posthumously awarded the Victoria Cross, the highest award for gallantry. He was 42, the most senior soldier to be killed. Pride in him helped to soften the blow for his family, but there was an undercurrent of carping. Had he acted too impetuously? Was it a commanding officer's place to be at the front? Was this a brand of heroism bordering on recklessness? A Channel 4 programme suggested that it was a 'virtual suicide attack'. It was not easy for his widow to remain impervious. She denounced the programme as outrageous.

'You will always get detractors,' she says patiently. 'It's sad that when we have something good, we look for a reason to undermine it. It's a rather British trait. We nibble away at the positive. I believe in what H did, and I think he was very brave. The advance had ground to a halt. Light was coming up. They were worried about the objective. What he achieved set the seal on the rest of the campaign. The Argentines appreciated that they were up against a much better enemy than they had thought and everybody was bucked up because we had that first victory, after several losses at sea. If you are a leader of men, that's where you are: at the front.'

Daily Telegraph, 2rd April 2012 [Colonel H Jones was at St Peter's School, Seaford, from 1949-53. His son was at the school at the time of his father's death.]

Diseases

The Black Death

The impact of the Black Death was very severe. There was huge loss of life from this plague that arrived from the sea, and ports like Seaford suffered first...

Survival in the middle ages was by no means guaranteed. Blatchington survived the Black Death, but it might easily not have done so. The three nearest villages to the east virtually disappeared, shrinking to the point where they became economically non-viable. Sutton-next-Seaford, Chyngton (or Chinting) and Exceat villages were each reduced to a single farm in the aftermath of the plague. Blatchington was lucky not to share their fate; it survived the crisis by the skin of its teeth.

Rodney Castleden, *On Blatchington Hill*

Smallpox

Seaford, 29th December 1755

...I hope by your next, which I shall expect very soon, to hear a good account of your little Nanny, as my Sister acquainted me she was taken with the Small Pox and in a hopeful way; may God be favourable to her and all your little ones, in that disagreeable and loathsome Distemper.

Letter from John Hubbersty to his brother Zachary, ESRO AMS 6126/13

Sometimes records of where [18th century] inoculations took place are missing. The Reverend Davies mentioned that Seaford was keen to follow Glynde's example; 'Mr Harrison inoculates his family and some friends in his house at Sutton, which leads to the inoculation of Seaford.' Mr Snelling was apparently to be the inoculator, but there is nothing to confirm where and when this occurred. Certainly some residents were treated by Daniel Sutton and, as described disapprovingly by Davies, sent back to the town before they were properly aired.

Diana Crook, *Defying the Demon, Smallpox in Sussex*

January 22 saw most of us safely back. The next day the majority were vaccinated because of the smallpox scare in the district. Several boys had been done at home, but there are always plenty of folk who believe in the good old Spanish custom of leaving the morrow to fend for itself. The scare is ancient history now but it is not too late to record our vote of thanks and appreciation to the local medical authorities in general, and Dr Sutton in particular, for the precautions they took and the tireless energy they showed to combat what could have become a very nasty problem.

King's Mead Terminal Letters, Easter Term 1951, SMA (Schools)

Malaria

Town flooded again – water should be got rid of quicker or in the summer it will cause malaria, many infectious diseases of the past summers can be put down to it.

27.7.1846 SMA (WEA1)

Measles

A large percentage of the School underwent a new experience today in being punctured in an unmentionable spot, as a preventive measure against measles. Some preferred to take their breakfast standing, and later, when the question of a School walk was mooted vice games, many became suddenly and disconcertingly lame.

…The next few days found the school departing upstairs with spots and temperatures. The grand total at one time reached 34. Many hands made light work and a cheerful acceptance of the necessary emergency.

King's Mead Terminal Letters, Easter Term 1938 and Christmas Term 1946, SMA (Schools)

Gradually two unwelcome strangers in our midst advertised their presence, the measle germ and that elusive little fiend, the streptococcus. This was an unholy alliance, because the one played into the hands of the other, and in this instance everything was in their favour. Only a handful of boys could be relied upon as being proof against measles, and with the other enemy there is, of course no such thing as immunity. In fact it is a case of once bitten, twice vulnerable. For the next six weeks life was certainly very intense. Meals had to be cooked in triplicate; the survivors downstairs were formed into pantry squads; the gallant Colonel, having no boys left in his form, was found peeling potatoes in the scullery; Mr Bell did everything that a schoolmaster is not expected to do, while Tony Gillet hunted the impertinent rabbit for the pot. Upstairs lunches were distributed in lightning fashion up and down Mind Your Head passage, Miss Clarke and Miss Greenaway breaking all records with their trays, while the Major, wedged tight into the narrow house-maid's cupboard, with his sleeves rolled up, was washing up the 'sick lunches' and cursing us playfully if we brought the implements in the wrong order. It seems futile to write about such things here, but this was the life of the school or a considerable part of it at the time.

St Peter's School Magazine, No 82, 1945, SMA (Schools)

Almshouses, Hospitals and Convalescent Homes

Almshouses [in Croft Lane]
The Rev JP Fitzgerald considered the present system of laws for relieving the indigent and aged poor, there is a scanty allowance from the Poor Rate, and they are often obliged to go and live in a Poor House, where husbands and wives are separated for the remainder of their days.

The Fitzgerald Charity was established to provide residences and maintenances for aged and infirm persons, being of the class of labouring poor, both male and female, and being not less than 60 years of age and of good character. The benefits of the Charity to be confined to such persons, as at the time of applying, shall have resided in some parish or place (except the town of Lewes) situate within nine miles as the crow flies from the parish church of Seaford, during the ten years immediately preceding the application.

Seaford Almshouses, SCM Vol 10, 1936

THE OUTDOOR BOYS

'We are outdoor boys,
We will go out-of-doors in all weathers,
We will leave the streets and go to the open fields,
We will bathe whenever we can; and learn to swim as soon as we
can,
We will wash our bodies daily with cold water,
We will clean our teeth,
We will sleep with open windows and lengthen our lives,
We will learn all we can from the lives of plants and animals,
We will write or draw some of the things that interest us,
We will open our eyes to the sky,
We will open our ears to the song of the wind,
We will open our hearts to our friends,
We will share all good things with others.'

Tide Mills Hospital School *Anthology*

Anyone who has ever been to the Heritage Craft Schools at Chailey and Tidemills, Bishopston, will agree with the Rt Hon Arthur Henderson when he described it as a national asset, and regretted that its work was not more widely known... Godfathers and godmothers of Tidemills attended the performance of a charming operetta by crippled boys, and perhaps most wonderful of all, was the display of Margaret Morris remedial movements by some of the bed-ridden boys.
The Gift of Tidemills, SCM January 1930, Vol 4

The buildings of the Marine Hospital School and Hospital, at Tidemills, on the coast, near Newhaven, began [in 1924] with the conversion of an Admiralty hut, and have since grown until they cover an area of nearly 30,000 square feet, and with the Nurses' Home have a total length of 582 feet, which is 100 feet more than the overall length of St Paul's Cathedral. Situated on a southern shore and actually within reach of the waves, a more ideal position for an orthopaedic centre could hardly be imagined. The solaria (or open concrete terraces for beds, etc.) extend for 400 feet along the south front, with an area of 6,500 square feet, and will when desired accommodate all the 100 beds from the wards, which can be wheeled out into the sun at a moment's notice...

Tidemills is, in itself, another type of lighthouse, guiding the crippled boys into the desired harbour of healthy independence. After operations at Chailey the boys are transferred to Tidemills to convalesce, and during the Christmas and summer holidays, when the Chailey schoolboys go home, those who are bedridden, or not considered fit to travel by the doctors, go to Tidemills and greatly benefit by the change of air and scene.

ALAS! THAT ALL THIS MUST NOW BE READ IN THE PAST TENSE, FOR DURING THE SECOND WORLD WAR THE ENTIRE UNIT WAS COMPLETELY AND ENTIRELY DESTROYED, AND NOT A TRACE OF THIS MOST NECESSARY AND LIVE PART OF THE BOYS' HERITAGE REMAINS.

But the foundations are still there, and the foundations and traditions of any and every place are what matter most. Before long it is hoped to see another Tidemills arise again to play its own particular part in the life of the Heritage boys.

Grace Kimmins, *Heritage, Craft Schools and Hospitals, Chailey, 1903–1948*

The Seaside Convalescent Hospital [demolished in 1964]
The story opens with four young men walking down Piccadilly late onc night in the year 1860. They found a poor ill woman crying upon a doorstep ... The hospital had discharged her that morning, and by evening, destitute and exhausted, she was crying helplessly by the roadside ... The next morning their steward was sent to the south coast to start house-hunting. The house, when bought, was to be staffed and equipped to look after relays of poor women, six at a time, who were to be sent there on discharge from the London hospitals, and given a seaside holiday. The house chosen was Tal-land House, High Street, Seaford, and there the scheme prospered for ten years. In 1870, the need being great and the accommodation small, new premises were sought [in Crouch Lane].

The architecture, when compared to buildings especially designed to fulfil the requirements of a modern convalescent home, leaves much to be desired. Still, however, although now under the National Health Scheme, it continues to take patients, both men and women, and give them two or three weeks holiday between their discharge from hospital and the full resumption of their working lives.

Few of the patients are now as destitute as the woman whose plight inspired the foundation of the hospital, though the lives of many are hard enough. There is no doubt of the benefit they derive from their visits, or of their appreciation of all that is done for them by the staff.

SJH, *The Story of a Hospital*, SCM Vol 27, 1953

Since its foundation in the year 1860 the hospital, according to its last year's report, has been the means of restoring to health nearly 17,000 persons of both sexes; of enabling fathers and breadwinners of families to return to their wage-earning occupations; mothers to go to their homes invigorated and restored to health, to the care of their children and households; and the young to resume their duties in offices, workshops, households, and schools.

Amongst these were some hundreds of cases of young persons in the early stages of consumption, who were completely restored to health by the invigorating air of Seaford and the care and good unlimited diet received at the hospital.

Descriptive Guide to Seaford, Newhaven and Vicinity, 189?

Seaside Convalescent Home, Seaford

Telsemure Childrens Convalesan Home [sic]
I was at the above in 1926 age just 15 yrs, with four other girls, all under 18 yrs, with a Sister and Matron. The children were I think from poor homes in London, each child was bathed and hair washed and inspected on arrieval [sic]; one little boy had out grown his vest and we had to cut it to get it off. One little girl had lost her leg above the knee and was in a pushchair, her name I remember was Lue Lue, some had spinal jackets. We were proud of our nurses uniforms, when taking the younger children in large wicker prams, seating 3 or 4 each side with feet in well in centre, along the prom-enade, if wet, play with them in building behind flint stone in Dane Road, it had a large stuffed bear on wheels, on which we would be able to give three or so children rides from end of room to the other. There were two large rooms, with iron cots on both sides; we all took turns to be on night duty; and had to keep awake or else!! And stoke boiler in cellar.

I had to go home to Newhaven after 7 months to look after my Mother; it was a year I think before I went back to work in Seaford, at a Miss Green's next to a Bank.

DA Honeywood

SMA (P6) [hand written account]

Deaths and Epitaphs

A shepherd was charged with sheep stealing at 'Chingtinge' [Chyngton]. He was found guilty and the sentence would normally have been one of death. However, the accused claimed 'the Benefit of the Clergy', and a Minister was sent for to hear him read from the Bible and to question the man on religious matters. Finally the court granted 'Benefit of the Clergy' and the sentence was commuted from death to branding on the left hand.

Edna and Mac McCarthy, *History Trail of the Town and Cinque Port of Seaford*

1773. James, son of Joseph and Elizabeth Stevens, killed by a sweep of Mr Washer's windmill
1796. Buried John Cosstick, accidentally killed by falling down the cliff, by endeavouring to take mews' eggs
David Arscott, *Dead and Buried in Sussex*, 2007

In the churchyard [Bishopstone] are groups of stone table-tombs with undecipherable inscriptions – the salty fingers of the sea winds have corroded them away – and sides that here and there have burst outwards, as though a weary ghost had pushed a head through to look upon the world again. Such tombs, especially when crooked and bulging, always make me think of that marvellous opening chapter of Walter de la Mare's novel *The Return*, and the green spider eyes that looked through the crack in the brickwork.

The prevailing families buried in the churchyard seem to be those of Catt and Venus – the latter, with a masculine Christian name before it, is rather surprising.
Esther Meynell, *Sussex Cottage*, 1936

IN PEACE
BENEATH THIS STONE REPOSES
HENRY TRACEY COXWELL
THE GREATEST OF ALL AERONAUTS
HIS ASCENTS INTO THE HEAVENS
WERE INNUMERABLE; AND ON 5TH
SEPTEMBER 1862 HE ATTAINED
TO THE GREAT HEIGHT OF MORE
THAN SEVEN MILES. HIS IS THE
HIGHEST POINT EVER REACHED BY
MAN. HAVING THUS IN LIFE
APPROACHED MORE NEARLY THAN
MORTAL THE GATES OF THE INFINITE
HE HAS NOW IN DEATH WITH A
TRUE AND STEDFAST FAITH PASSED
THROUGH INTO REST EVERLASTING

Seaford Cemetery epitaph to Henry Coxwell, 1819–1900, balloonist

Among graves in the [St Peter's] churchyard are those of Robert Lambe, a local farmer on whose land much of Claremont Road was built in 1879, as an inland by-pass away from the eroded seaside route to the west. Also buried here are Dr William Tyler Smith who came to Seaford in 1857 intending to develop it into 'a second Brighton', Thomas Anstey Guthrie who, as F Anstey, wrote a popular Victorian novel *Vice Versa* and a number of soldiers from the eighteenth-century Blatchington Barracks, and their families.
Patricia Berry, *Seaford Memories 1950–1999*

All Souls

In forgotten corners
Lost in a wreck of leaves,
Shaded by sycamore shrouds,
Draped in ivy's widow weeds
They lie neglected;
Someone's husband or wife,
Concealed testimonies
To the littleness of life.

Peter Martin, extract from *Ghost Music*

The Seaford Seven Sisters

SEA

EXERCISE

AIR

FISHING

OZONE

RAMBLES

DOWNS

Sunny Seaford, Official Publicity Bureau, 1936

BIBLIOGRAPHY

Books and pamphlets consulted for extracts and research

Abbreviations:

ESCL	East Sussex County Library
ESRO	East Sussex Record Office
OUP	Oxford University Press
SAS	Sussex Archaeological Society
SCM	Sussex County Magazine
SMA	Seaford Museum Archives
SRC	Sussex Record Society
U of S	University of Sussex

Aldsworth, Fred and Freke, David, *Historic Towns in Sussex, an archaeological survey*, Institute of Archaeology, University of London, 1976

Arscott, David, *Explore Sussex, Its Coast, Countryside and Heritage*, Local Heritage Books, 1986

Arscott, David, *The Sussex Story*, Pomegranate Press, 1992

Arscott, David, *Dead and Buried in Sussex*, Pomegranate Press, 2007

Askaroff, Alex I, *Patches of Heaven*, Vol 1, Crows Nest Publications, 2001

Astell, Joan A, *To the Independent Electors of Seaford*, Pt II, the Middle Years of Seaford's Parliamentary Story 1768-1786, 1973

Banks, W, *Seaford: Past and Present. Handbook and Visitors' Guide*, 1892

Beckett, Arthur, *The Spirit of the Downs*, Methuen & Co Ltd, 1949

Berry, Patricia, *Seaford Memories 1950–1999*, S B Publications, 2003

Black's Guide to Sussex, 1861

Boodle, Ethel CM, *Seaford*, SCM Vol 1, 1927

Brandon, Peter, *The Sussex Landscape*, Hodder & Stoughton, 1974

Brandon, Peter, *The Discovery of Sussex*, Phillimore, 2010

Carter, Agnes H, *A Canteen in a Canadian Camp* (1917), SCM Vol 8 1934

Castleden, Rodney, *On Blatchington Hill, History of a Downland Village*, Blatchington Press, 2011

Chambers, Miss Amy, *Log Book 1890–1928*, Infants' School, Church Street, Seaford, SMA

Chambers, George F, *A Tourist's Guide to the County of Sussex*, 1891

Coppin, Paul, *101 Medieval Churches of East Sussex*, SB Publications 2001

Coulcher, Patrick, *Unto the Hills*, The Book Guild, 2001

Crawford, The Rev G.P., *Seaford in Parliament 1660–1832*, SCM Vol 5, 1931

Crook, Diana, *Defying the Demon, Smallpox in Sussex*, Dale House Press, 2006

Dennis, Robert Nathaniel, *Notes on Sussex Ornithology*, ed. W.H. Mullens and N.F. Ticehurst, HFG Wetherby, 1925

Dennis, Robert Nathaniel, Diaries 1846–1869, *The Bird Man of Blatchington,* ed Rodney Castleden, Blatchington Press, 2011

Descriptive Guide to Seaford, Newhaven and Vicinity, South Counties Press 1890

East Sussex Police 1840–1967, SMA (LO)

Ellman, Rev Edward Boys, *Recollections of a Sussex Parson*, Combridges, 1925

Evans, Rev AA, *A Christmas Fight Off Seaford Head*, SCM Vol 1, 1926–7

Farrant, John H, *Sussex Depicted, Views and Descriptions 1600–1800,* SRC Vol 85, 2001

Fellows, Peter, *A Short History of a local Seaplane Station 1917–1920*, 2001

Gordon, Kevin, *From A Seaford Album*, Sussex Express & County Herald

Gordon, Kevin, *Seaford Through Time*, Amberley Publishing, 2010

Green, Ivan, *The Book of the Cinque Ports*, Barracuda Books, 1984

Horsfield, TW, *The History of Sussex*, Baxter 1835

Hudson, WH, *Nature in Downland*, JM Dent, 1923

Hughes, Wendy, *Shipwrecks of Sussex*, The History Press, 2011

Hyndman, Henry Mayers, *The Record of an Adventurous Life*, 1911

Johnson, WH, *Sussex Disasters*, SB Publications, 1998

Johnson, WH, *A Grim Almanack of Sussex*, Sutton Publishing, 2007

Kidner, RW, *The Newhaven and Seaford Branch*, The Oakwood Press, 1979

Kimmins, Grace T, *Heritage, Craft Schools and Hospitals, Chailey, 1903–1948*, The Baynard Press, 1948

King's Mead Terminal Letters, 1927–1960 SMA (Schools)

Lawrie, Rose Mary, *The Heritage Craft Schools, Chailey*, SCM Vol 25, 1951

Lewis, Marie, *A Brief History of Seaford*, ESCL, 1982

Longstaff-Tyrrell, Peter, *The Seaford Mutiny of 1795*, Gote House Publishing Co, 2001

Lower, MA, *Memorials of the Town, Parish, and Cinque-Port of Seaford*, SAS VII, John Russell, 1858

Lower, MA. *The Worthies of Sussex*, J Richards. SAS Collections No 7, 1856

Lower, MA & Cooper, WD, *Further Memorials of Seaford*, SAS Vol XVII, 1865

Lower, MA, *Notes on Seaford*, Lewes: GP Bacon, 1868

Lowerson, John, ed. *An Embryonic Brighton? Victorian and Edwardian Seaford*, U of S 1975

McCarthy, Edna and Mac, *History Trail of the Town and Cinque Port of Seaford*, Lindel Organisation, c 1970

McCarthy, Edna and Mac, *Sussex River, Seaford to Newhaven*, Lindel Organisation, 1975

McPhee, Bruce Alexander, *Works Driver, a view of SOUTHDOWN from the inside*, 2001

Mantell, Gideon, *Journals, 1818–1852*, OUP, 1940

Martin, Peter, *Ghost Music*, Seacroft Arts, 2010

Mee, Arthur, *Sussex*, Hodder & Stoughton, 1937

Meredith, George, *The Letters of*, ed. CL Cline, Vol 1, Oxford 1970

Meredith, George, *Short Stories, The House on the Beach*, 1920

Meynell, Esther, *Sussex Cottage*, Chapman & Hall, 1936

Meynell, Esther, *Sussex*, Robert Hale, 1945

Moore, Judy, *Silly Sussex*, SB Publications, 2004

Nairn, Ian & Pevsner, Nikolaus, *Sussex, The Buildings of England*, Harmondsworth : Penguin, 1965

Odam, John, *Bygone Seaford*, Seaford Museum and Heritage Society, 1990, reprinted 2009

Odam, John (In association with Brigid Chapman) *The Seaford Story, 1000–2000 AD*, SB Publications, 1999

Patmore, Coventry, *Hastings, Lewes, Rye and the Sussex Marshes*, George Bell, 1887

Redman, Joan EV, A *Pint Pot of Old Seaford*, ESCL

Ridley, Katharine H, *Schools in Seaford, East Sussex*, Dissertation, Durham University 1984, SMA

St Leonard's & St Luke's Churches, Seaford, *Magazine*, Mar/Apr 2011

St Peter's School Magazine 1927–1979

Seaford, A Member of the Cinque Ports Liberty of Hastings, Seaford Museum

Seaford Baptist Church, 1899–1973, The Lindel Organisation, 1974

Seaford Parish Magazine

Seaford Scene

A Seaford Sketchbook, The Drawings of HH Evans 1849–1926, S B Publications, 2001

Seaford Timeline, Seaford Museum and Heritage Society, 2002

Seaford Town Council *Newsletter*, Issue 19, April 2008

Seaford Town Football Club, http://www.stfc.org.uk/aboutl.htm

Simpson, Jacqueline, *Folklore of Sussex*, The History Press, 2009

SJH, *The Story of a Hospital*, SCM, Vol 27, 1953

Stuart, Morley, *Memories of a Seaford Model Parliament*, SCM Vol 20, 1946

Sunny Seaford, Sussex. Official Register. Official Publicity Bureau, 1936

Talbot, Bruce and Weaver, Paul, *Flight of the Martlets, The Golden Age of Sussex Cricket*, Breedon Books Publishing, 2008

Turner, Thomas, *Diary, 1754–1765*, ed. David Vaisey, OUP, 1985

Turnor, Reginald, *Sussex*, Paul Elek, 1947

Victoria History of the Counties of England – Sussex, Constable, 1905

The War In East Sussex, Sussex Express & County Herald, August 1945

Whatmore, LE, *St Lewinna: East Sussex Martyr*, 1979

White, Charles, *Autobiography – Local Detective*, SMA (LO)

Willett, Rev Frederick, *The Tide-Mill, Bishopston*, SCM Vol 8, 1934

Wynter, WR, *Old Seaford*, Farncombe & Co Ltd, 1922

Newspapers and magazines

Brighton Gazette
Daily News
Daily Telegraph
Derby Mercury
Evening News
Hull Daily Mail
The Illustrated London News
Lloyd's Weekly Newspaper
London Globe
Morning Post
The Penny Illustrated Paper
Picture House (Magazine of the Cinema Theatre Association)
Seaford Gazette
The Spectator
The Star
Sussex Daily News
Sussex Express and County Herald
Sussex Weekly Advertiser and Lewes Journal
The Times

Index

The Beach, Seaford

Other books written and edited by Diana Crook

The Ladies of Miller's, Dale House Press 1996

A Reader's Choice, Selections from books by Julian Fane, Dale House Press 1996

A Lewes Diary 1916–44 by Mrs Henry Dudeney, Tartarus Press 1998

A Peculiar Devotion: The friendship of Sir Philip Sassoon and Mrs Henry Dudeney, Dale House Press 1999

A Box of Toys – An Anthology of Lewes Writings, Dale House Press 2004

Defying the Demon – Smallpox in Sussex, Dale House Press 2006

Ragged Lands – Viscountess Wolseley's College for Lady Gardeners, Glynde, Dale House Press 2008

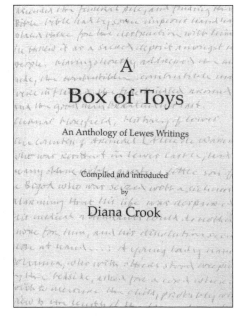